Glisk

Moments of grace in leadership and life

Dr Stephen Duns

Contents

Introduction

There are moments in life and leadership that arrive carrying a choice.

Sometimes the choice is obvious and urgent. Something is broken, a decision is required and perhaps action matters. At other times, the choice is so subtle it barely registers; a pause taken or missed, a question asked or withheld or even a raised eyebrow or a deep sigh. A moment when we move too quickly or stay just long enough for something else to come into view.

These moments don't usually announce themselves with a drum roll. More often, they arrive disguised as ordinary; another meeting, conversation or tired evening when you tell yourself you'll think about it tomorrow.

These are the moments this book is interested in.

Not because they are dramatic or demand action, but because the way we meet them shapes what becomes possible next. Some choices close things down, others open space. Some lead to efficiency, resolution and the comforting sense of a job well done. Others, more quietly, allow grace to visit. Sometimes the most efficient response turns out to be the one that costs us the most.

The word *glisk* comes from Old Scots. It refers to a brief glimpse of light, a flash of understanding, a momentary opening or the gentle warmth of embers of a fire. A glisk does not last. It cannot be summoned or held. It appears and disappears, often before we fully realise what we've seen. It's the leadership equivalent of thinking, "Oh… that," and then watching it slip away as you return to your inbox.

But once glimpsed, it alters our sense of what is possible.

In this book, Glisk names those moments when a different way of responding becomes visible. When power and love briefly come back into a relationship. When we notice the urge to fix or decide and choose, instead, to stay present a little longer, when the choice we make or fail to notice we are making, quietly shifts the direction of a conversation, a relationship, a system or an inner life.

Grace, as it appears here, is not a moral achievement or a spiritual accomplishment. It is not about being right, good or especially evolved. Grace is not something we can produce on demand, no matter how many leadership programs we've completed or books we've read. It emerges, sometimes unexpectedly, when the conditions allow it, often briefly, imperfectly, at some personal cost and occasionally at an inconvenient moment.

This book is not a guide to making the right choices.

It will not offer steps, models or techniques. It will not tell you how to ensure grace appears or how to get it right. There is no checklist, no framework and no final chapter where everything comes together neatly and you feel quietly superior to your former self.

That absence is deliberate.

When we are under pressure, overloaded or anxious, it is natural to reach for instruction. We want clarity, certainty and something to lean on. We want to know what works, how others have solved this already, so we can do the same, preferably before lunch.

But the moments this book is concerned with are rarely resolved well by formula. Any attempt to reduce them to method risks turning presence into performance and grace into something we try to manage. And grace, as you will notice, is not something we can manage.

What matters more than technique in these moments is presence. Presence is not insight, empathy or wisdom.

Presence is capacity. The capacity to notice what is happening in us and around us before we act; to feel the pull toward certainty without obeying it automatically, to remain available to intensity without absorbing it and to hold suffering, joy, frustration and care without immediately trying to tidy them away.

Presence shapes choice and choice in these moments, shapes consequence.

This book offers stories rather than instruction because presence cannot be taught in the usual way. It has to be experienced. Each chapter is an invitation to inhabit a moment and notice what happens in you as it unfolds. Some stories show grace arriving and others show it being missed. In several, the difference is almost imperceptible until later, when you find yourself thinking, "Ah. That was the moment." That, too, is intentional.

In real life, we rarely know in the moment whether we are opening something up or closing it down. Often, we only realise afterwards, when the field has shifted and something can no longer be retrieved. Occasionally, this realisation arrives with insight, sometimes it arrives with a wince or a rueful laugh.

You might find yourself wanting more explanation as you read. Wanting to know what to do differently next time, how to respond better and how to avoid the miss. That desire makes sense. It is part of how many of us have learned to survive complexity and be seen as competent while doing so.

This book does not meet that desire directly. Instead, it invites you to notice it, to notice the urge to act, to decide, to simplify or to bring things to an end. To notice the relief that comes with narrowing options and the discomfort of staying with ambiguity. These impulses are not flaws, they are human. They are the organism doing its best to manage what feels like too much, usually with the very best of intentions.

Grace often asks something else. It asks for a different quality of attention, a willingness to stay with the moment long enough to sense what is actually being asked. Sometimes that leads to action, restraint or an awkward pause you wish would hurry up. The difference is not the behaviour itself, but the consciousness from which it arises.

This is not a book about leadership as a role or position, though many of the stories are drawn from that world.

Leadership appears here as a way of being with power, love, loss, limits and responsibility across a whole life. In that sense, the territory of this book extends beyond organisations into families, friendships, intimate relationships and inner experience, often into places where no one is particularly impressed by your title.

You will not be persuaded or instructed by this book. You are invited instead to keep company with these moments. To notice where you feel yourself lean forward and where you want the story to hurry up or resolve itself. To sense where a choice is being made, even if it is not yet named and occasionally to smile at how familiar these patterns are.

If grace appears while reading, it will not be because the book has explained it well. It will be because something in you recognised the moment and chose, perhaps only briefly, to stay.

That is enough.

That is the work.

Collection I — Power and Love

Power and love are not themes in this collection so much as forces you have already met, often before you had words for them.

Power is the part of you that can say yes, say no, set direction or hold a line to protect what matters. Love is the part of you that can stay close, listen, include, repair or soften what has become defended. Most of us learned to separate them. We are rewarded for one in certain moments and cautioned against it in others. We learn which parts of ourselves are safe to bring forward and which should remain quietly in the background.

As we enter this space, there is a simple truth that most of us would rather step around.

Life hurts.

Not always loudly and not always in ways we can name. But the first truth of being human, as Buddhism teaches us, is that we suffer. We suffer by carrying sorrow, fear, disappointment, shame, loneliness and fatigue. We carry it in our bodies, in our stories and in the places we have adapted to belong. Organisations carry it too, as do families, teams, couples and communities. Systems don't leave suffering at the door, they reorganise around it by hiding, denying, managing and projecting it.

Often, without meaning to, we look for someone who can hold what the whole cannot. Sometimes we call that person the leader. Sometimes it is the eldest daughter, the competent manager, the calm partner or the one who can "handle things", the one who doesn't fall apart. The system leans and the person absorbs, not because they are weak, but because they are available.

This first collection begins at that inflexion point, where power and love start to drift apart or find each other again. It is not always dramatic. Sometimes it looks like a firm boundary that is clean rather than cruelor or care that does not overreach. It can be a moment of authority that settles instead of tightens or a moment of tenderness that keeps its shape.

Power and love are the two forces we reach for when life gets real. Power gives us agency. It says we can act, decide, protect, name, draw boundaries and move. Love gives us connection. It says we can stay close, care, include, soften, listen and belong. Many of the moments that strain us most do not ask us to choose between them, they ask us to hold both at once.

Trouble arises not because power or love are present, but because they fall out of a relationship.

Power without love can harden into control, certainty, domination or a kind of efficiency that leaves people smaller. Love without power can dissolve into over accommodation, avoidance, rescuing or a tenderness that quietly abandons truth. Neither is enough on its own.

Grace seems to visit when power and love come back into the relationship. Not perfectly, not permanently, but briefly and unmistakably. A tone softens without losing clarity, a boundary is set without contempt, a truth is spoken without a need to win or someone stays present to intensity without absorbing it, allowing room to breathe again.

These chapters are meant to be read as entries, not lessons. Each one holds a particular flavour of the same human question, what happens when strength and care have to share the same moment. You might recognise yourself in one chapter more than another. You might feel resistant, relieved, irritated or seen. You might notice your own preferences, the places you lean toward control, accommodation or disappearance.

None of that is a problem. It is information.

This book is not trying to teach you how to make grace appear. Not because it is unimportant, but because it is not a technique. It is a capacity. It grows through moments, through failure, through return and through the small choices you make when you feel yourself tightening or disappearing.

If there is anything to notice as you move through this first collection, it is simply this. When power and love fall out of a relationship, something in us contracts. When they return to a relationship, even briefly, something in us has room to breathe.

You might like to read like you are sitting down beside your own life, not standing above it. You do not need to agree with anything here. You only need to notice what happens in you as you meet these two forces again, power and love and how often grace has been trying to find a place to land.

One:

Holding Power Without Hardening

When authority tightens under pressure

The meeting had been scheduled for ninety minutes. By the time people arrived, most already knew it would run long.

There had been weeks of accumulated strain. Targets were slipping, external scrutiny had sharpened and emails had become careful and clipped. Conversations were happening elsewhere, rarely in the room where decisions were meant to be made.

People took their seats with quiet efficiency. Laptops opened or notebooks aligned. A joke was offered, smiled at and left there. Someone cleared their throat. The air felt slightly compressed.

At the head of the table sat Amina, a senior executive, a woman who had learned how to carry pressure with a steady face. She was aware of the weight of expectation in the room. This meeting mattered and a decision needed to be made. The agenda was followed closely; updates were given, risks named and options outlined. Nothing about the process looked unreasonable. From the outside, it would have appeared competent and contained.

Inside Amina's body, something was tightening.

A subtle constriction in the chest, a shortening of breath and an impatience with complexity. The sense that time was being wasted and clarity was slipping away. As one explanation lengthened, Amina interrupted, just slightly. When a question wandered, it was redirected. When hesitation appeared, she completed the thought and moved on.

No one objected, they adjusted. Voices softened, contributions became safer and people spoke in ways that were accurate rather than alive. The room grew quieter, not with focus but with compliance.

Near the end of the table, Dev, a non-binary program lead, paused mid-sentence. Looked down and looked up again. Amina noticed the pause and felt the familiar urge to press on. The agenda was already behind.

"Let's keep moving," she said, evenly. "We can't afford to stall here."

The decision was made ten minutes later. It was defensible, logical and on paper, it made sense. The meeting ended on time. As people left, there was a sense of relief mixed with something else. A dullness. A faint disappointment that no one quite named. Emails followed confirming actions. The system moved on.

The consequences emerged slowly: resistance surfaced later in private, implementation stalled and trust thinned a little more. No single moment could be blamed. Nothing had gone obviously wrong.

--- o ---

The meeting had been scheduled for ninety minutes. By the time people arrived, most already knew it would run long.

There had been weeks of accumulated strain. Targets were slipping. External scrutiny had sharpened. Emails had become careful and clipped. Conversations were happening elsewhere, rarely in the room where decisions were meant to be made.

People took their seats with quiet efficiency. Laptops opened or notebooks aligned. A joke was offered, smiled at and left there. Someone cleared their throat. The air felt slightly compressed.

At the head of the table sat Amina, a senior executive, a woman who had learned how to carry pressure with a steady face. She was aware of the weight of expectation in the room. This meeting mattered and a decision needed to be made.

The agenda was followed closely; updates were given, risks named and options outlined. Nothing about the process looked unreasonable. From the outside, it would have appeared competent and contained.

Inside Amina's body, something was tightening. A subtle constriction in the chest, a shortening of breath and an impatience with complexity. The sense that time was being wasted and clarity was slipping away.

As one explanation lengthened, Amina felt the impulse to interrupt. She noticed it. She did not suppress it. She simply stayed with the sensation for a moment longer than usual.

When a question wandered, she felt the urge to redirect. She noticed that too.

The room was quiet in the same way. People were careful, voices were measured.

Near the end of the table, Dev, a non-binary program lead, paused mid-sentence. Looked down and looked up again.

Amina waited, not long, just long enough to feel exposed.

"I'm not sure this is the right time to say this," Dev said, "but I think we're all more exhausted than we're admitting."

The words landed without drama. A few people nodded. Someone leaned back and another exhaled slowly. Nothing else happened for a moment.

Amina felt the pull to respond quickly. To reassure, move back to the agenda and convert the moment into action. She noticed that pull and did not follow it.

"Yes," she said. "I think that's true."

The meeting continued, the decision was still made and the constraints were still real. But something had shifted. People spoke with more candour, disagreement surfaced without sharpness and responsibility began to spread rather than concentrate. The decision was not perfect, no one pretended it was, but it held; implementation moved more smoothly and conversations continued in the open rather than in corridors.

Nothing about this outcome could be traced to a single

clever move, no technique had been applied and no authority had been relinquished. Only a moment had been noticed, a tightening felt and a pause taken and a space allowed to open. This is how power sometimes hardens and how sometimes it does not.

You might recognise both versions, perhaps even from the same day. You might notice what you feel when authority tightens, where you sense it first or what becomes possible when you stay with that sensation rather than act on it.

There is nothing here to resolve, just a difference to notice and perhaps, next time, to feel a little sooner.

Two:

Caring Without Disappearing

Love, boundaries and the quiet cost of over-accommodation

The request came late in the afternoon, not dramatic and not unreasonable. Just one more thing. The message was carefully worded. Appreciative, acknowledging how busy things were and emphasising how much it would help. It landed in the familiar way these things often do, carrying more weight than the words alone suggested.

Niroshini read it once, then again. She cared about this person, the team and the work. That had never been in question. Care was not something she had to manufacture. It came naturally, sometimes too naturally. She felt the familiar pull almost immediately. A slight tightening behind the eyes, a small shift in posture and the sense of leaning forward internally, even while sitting still.

Of course, I can make this work. She typed a quick reply; warm, reassuring and flexible.

"No problem. Happy to help."

The relief was immediate, on the other end and perhaps, in

the moment here too. The discomfort eased, the relationship felt intact, generous and kind.

The cost arrived later. It showed up that evening as fatigue that felt heavier than expected. The sense of having given something away without quite noticing when. The slight irritation that followed, aimed nowhere and everywhere at once. In the days that followed, the pattern repeated with more small requests, more adjustments and more quiet accommodations. Each one is defensible, minor and taken in the name of care.

Nothing was said. Niroshini remained available, supportive, appreciated and gradually less present to herself. Decisions began to feel harder, resentment flickered at odd moments and the care that had once felt expansive began to feel thin.

From the outside, it looked like commitment. From the inside, it felt like erosion. No boundary had been crossed dramatically, no one had demanded too much and there was no single moment to point to. Just a slow disappearing.

--- o ---

The request came late in the afternoon. Not dramatic. Not unreasonable. Just one more thing. The message was carefully worded. Appreciative, acknowledging how busy things were and emphasising how much it would help. It landed with the same familiar weight.

Niroshini read it once, then again. She cared about this person, the team and the work. That had never been in question. Care was not scarce. It flowed easily.

And she noticed something else. A slight tightening behind the eyes, a subtle leaning forward and the impulse to smooth things over before discomfort had time to settle.

She did not respond immediately. She stayed with the sensation, not analysing it, just noticing. The pull to accommodate, the wish to be helpful and the faint fear of disappointing someone they respected.

The pause was brief. Almost invisible.

When she replied, the tone was still warm. Still respectful. "I want to help," she wrote. "And I'm at capacity right now. Let's look together at what can wait or who else might support this."

There was a moment of uncertainty after sending it. A

flicker of doubt. Had she been selfish? Too firm? Risked something unnecessary?

The response came later than usual. "Thank you for saying that," it read. "I didn't realise how full things were. Let's talk."

The conversation that followed was not dramatic. No one apologised, no one was blamed. Something simply shifted. Expectations recalibrated, responsibility widened and the work continued.

Niroshini felt tired that evening but not depleted. The care was still there, intact and no longer leaking away unnoticed. Nothing about this moment would stand out in a report. No policy had changed or values were proclaimed. Yet something had been preserved.

This is the quiet edge where love can turn into disappearance. Care without boundaries does not usually announce itself as a problem. It looks generous, feels relational and is often praised. But over time, love without shape begins to cost more than it gives as it drains presence, erodes authority and leaves resentment where care once lived. Boundaries, when they come from attention rather than defence, do not diminish love. They allow it to remain whole.

You might recognise both versions of this moment. The one where care smooths things over and slowly thins you out and the one where care pauses long enough to include you, too. You might notice where you accommodate most quickly, what you feel just before you say yes and what happens when you let that feeling be there without acting on it.

There is nothing here to resolve, just a difference to feel and perhaps, next time, to notice sooner.

Three:

When Strength and Tenderness Meet

A moment when neither led alone

The conversation had been delayed more than once. Not avoided exactly, just deferred, each time with a reason that made sense. A full calendar, a sense that things might settle on their own or the hope that the moment would pass without needing to be named. It didn't.

By the time Sahar sat down with Minh, the air already carried the weight of what had been circling between them. Nothing had been said directly, but both of them knew this was not a routine check-in. Something had reached its limit.

Sahar was Minh's manager. A woman in her forties who had a reputation for being fair, steady and hard to rattle. People often described her as calm, but she knew the truth was more ordinary than that. She was not calm by nature. She had simply learned, sometimes the hard way, that if she moved too quickly, she would either soften the truth into meaninglessness or harden it into harm.

Minh arrived a few minutes late, apologising as he slid into the chair. A man in his early thirties, smart, diligent and liked by his peers. The kind of person who said yes quickly and meant it. The kind of person who carried more than anyone realised until it started to show.

Sahar waited until Minh had settled. She noticed his hands, the way they kept touching the edge of his notebook, straightening it as if alignment could keep things under control.

She had spent time with the question of whether this conversation was truly necessary. She had turned it over in her mind while driving home, while rinsing dishes and while lying awake at night with the familiar discomfort of knowing she was about to disappoint someone. That question had resolved itself. What needed to be said could no longer remain unspoken without doing damage. There was strength in that knowing. A steadiness that came from having looked away and looked back again.

There was also care. Genuine care for the person sitting opposite her. She knew what Minh had carried this past quarter, the workload had not been clean and some of the expectations set above him were unreasonable. She also knew something in his performance had shifted and the shift was now affecting other people.

To carry both at once required attention.

Sahar began slowly. "Minh, I want to talk about something that's been building for a while," she said. "Not a single incident. A pattern."

She let the words land. Minh's face stayed neutral, but his shoulders lifted slightly, just enough to register. His eyes flicked to the window, then back.

Sahar kept her voice plain. "I've noticed tasks slipping past deadlines more often. I've noticed decisions being held longer than they need to be and then made in a rush. I've noticed follow-up that doesn't happen unless someone reminds you twice." She paused. "And I've noticed the team starting to compensate for that, quietly."

Minh's mouth opened, then closed again. His hands folded, unfolded, then folded once more, as if they were trying to decide what posture to take.

Sahar felt the familiar impulse to reassure him. To say something kind, to soften the edge so the room could relax. She could already hear the kind of sentence she used to reach for. You're doing so much. It's understandable. It was true. It was also not the point, at least not yet.

She noticed the impulse and did not follow it. The truth still needed to be held.

Minh nodded once, quickly, as if the nod could be used to close the topic down. "I know," he said. "It's been a tough few months."

Sahar felt another impulse rise in her, a tightening and the desire to push through, to be absolutely clear, to make sure there was no room left for misunderstanding and to protect the organisation, the team and herself from the discomfort of ambiguity. She noticed that too.

She slowed instead. "Tell me what's happening for you," she said and even as she asked it, she could feel how easily this question could become an escape hatch, a way of making the conversation about feelings rather than impact.

Minh's gaze dropped to the table. He stared at a faint scratch in the laminate as if it were an important document. "I'm trying to keep up," he said, but the words came out flat, like a line he'd used before. "I'm working hard."

Sahar believed him. She could see it; the slightly hollow look around the eyes, the tension in the jaw, the way his laughter had become less frequent in the last month and the way his emails sometimes arrived at midnight with a brightness that didn't match the hour.

A part of her wanted to say, stop, take leave and step back. Fix yourself. Another part knew that would be a kind of rescue. It would bypass something more difficult and more true.

She stayed with the moment.

"Minh," she said, "I'm not questioning your effort." His head lifted slightly, as if bracing for the next sentence. "I'm naming the impact," she continued. "Because the impact is now landing on other people." Minh's face tightened. His eyes flashed with something like shame or anger or both. The line between them is often thin. "I didn't realise..." he began, then stopped.

Sahar watched the stop. She could feel the energy. The old familiar energy that appears in these conversations, made of pride and fear, where people want to be good and where the possibility of not being good feels like falling. She felt her own body respond. A small constriction in her chest, the reflex to move it along and to fill the silence with something efficient.

She leaned back slightly instead of leaning in. "I want to pause here," she said. "I can see this is landing heavily." The words were simple, unadorned. They did not offer rescue and they did not retreat.

Something shifted.

Minh exhaled. Not dramatically. Just enough to be felt. His shoulders dropped a fraction. He looked up and met Sahar's gaze for the first time since the conversation began. "I don't disagree," he said after a while. His voice was quieter now. "I just didn't realise how far it had gone."

A silence followed and this time it was not tense. It had weight, but also space. The kind of silence where something is being rearranged internally, piece by piece. Sahar felt the urge to fill it, to outline next steps, to make things feel safer by making them clearer and to convert this moment into a plan so she could leave the room feeling like she had done her job.

She let the urge pass.

Minh rubbed his thumb along the edge of the notebook again, slower now. "I think I've been... trying to do it all alone," he said, as if he were surprised by his own sentence.

"Like if I just push harder, it'll come right."

Sahar nodded once, small.

"And I haven't wanted to admit I can't," Minh added. The words were close to something tender. They hovered near the edge of what he would usually reveal.

Sahar felt tenderness in herself and also firmness. She needed both. "I hear that," she said. "And we need to change what's happening."

Minh nodded again. "I want to," he said. "I'm just not sure how yet."

Sahar noticed what happened in her own body when he said that. A loosening, not relief exactly, more a sense that the conversation had found its ground. That it had not tipped into collapse or control. They stayed on that ground.

They talked for a while longer about what Minh could stop carrying, what he could delegate without it feeling like failure, what he needed to name earlier, before it became a scramble, expectations, limits, what support might look like and what could not continue as it had been. Some things remained unresolved. Others were left deliberately open. Not because Sahar was avoiding clarity, but because she could feel that premature clarity would be another kind of tightening. A way to escape the discomfort of staying in what was real.

Nothing was fixed in that hour, no plan was finalised and no guarantees were made. But something essential had happened.

Sahar left feeling tired, but intact. Not drained and not inflated. Minh left quieter than when he had arrived, thoughtful, as if he were carrying less performance and more truth.

In the weeks that followed, the work was uneven. Old habits resurfaced. There were days when Minh did better and days when he slipped back into over-functioning, staying late and saying yes too quickly. There were moments of frustration and moments when he named things early, before they became crises and Sahar felt something in the system settle slightly, as if it had been holding its breath.

The relationship stretched and recalibrated - but it held.

Looking back later, Sahar could see that the content of the conversation mattered less than how it had been held. Not strength alone, not tenderness alone, but the willingness to remain with both, without allowing either to take over.

You might recognise this kind of moment, where clarity is required and care cannot be sacrificed. Where softening too much would betray the truth and where hardening would break something fragile and necessary.

You might notice what it takes in you to remain there, what pulls you toward force and what pulls you toward retreat.

There is nothing here to resolve, just a place to stay for a while.

Or the conversation you might have been deferring, with reasons that make perfect sense and yet keep the truth waiting.

Four:

The Fear Beneath Control

What power is often protecting?

It began in a way that hardly seemed worth noticing at the time. A door is closing with a little more force than necessary. Not a slam, just enough to register. Enough to carry something unspoken down the hallway.

Farid was in the kitchen, rinsing a cup, when he heard it. The sound landed somewhere in his body before it reached his mind. A tightening in the chest and a familiar heat rising behind the eyes. He paused with his hands under the tap, listening to the water run a moment longer than usual.

His son, Amir, had been like this lately. Quieter and more guarded. When he did speak, his words sometimes carried a sharpness that seemed out of proportion to the moment. Thirteen years old and already moving into a territory Farid could feel but not yet read. He dried his hands slowly and walked down the hallway. Not hurried, not calm either. The space between the kitchen and the bedroom felt longer than usual, as if something was gathering with each step.

He knocked once, lightly, then opened the door without

waiting.

Amir sat on the bed, shoulders slightly hunched, headphones resting around his neck. One foot tapped against the carpet in a steady rhythm. His eyes stayed on the floor.

"What was that about?" Farid asked. He kept his voice level. He had learned how much that mattered.

"Nothing," Amir said. The word was quiet, almost flat, but it carried weight. Not defiance exactly, more like distance and a closing in.

Farid felt irritation rise, quick and familiar. He had been patient all day, he had tried to give space and he was tired in a way that went beyond lack of sleep. He could feel the conversation slipping away from him and with it his sense of being connected, involved, still relevant.

"Don't talk to me like that," he said. "If something's wrong, you need to say it."

Amir shrugged, barely perceptible, still looking down.

In that moment, something tightened.

Not consciously, not strategically, just a gathering of energy that wanted direction. Farid stepped further into the room, his posture straightened and his voice took on a firmer edge, not raised, just unmistakably parental.

"I'm your dad," he said. "You don't get to shut me out." The words landed heavily in the small space between them. Amir's shoulders lifted, then set. His jaw tightened. Without looking up, he reached for his headphones and pulled them back over his ears, turning slightly away.

"That's exactly what I mean," he muttered. The room felt smaller now. The air is thicker.

Farid stood there, heart beating faster than he wanted to admit, unsure what to do next. Part of him wanted to escalate, to insist on engagement, to remove the headphones and force the conversation into the open. Another part of him wanted to retreat, to leave the room and pretend this moment had not happened, to avoid making it worse.

Both impulses came from the same place.

Fear.

Fear that he was losing touch with his son. Fear that something important was happening inside this young person and he was already behind. Fear that if he did not assert himself now, the distance would widen beyond repair.

He had not expected parenting to feel like this. He had imagined guidance, teaching and shared activity. He had not imagined this steady ache of uncertainty, this sense that love itself made him vulnerable. Control, in that moment, felt like protection. Like the only available way to hold onto what mattered. He remained standing for a few seconds longer, then noticed his own body. The shallow breath, the clenched hands and the way his shoulders were braced as if for impact.

He realised that he was no longer trying to understand Amir. He was trying to quiet his own alarm. The recognition did not dissolve the fear. It did not make the situation clearer. But it slowed him down. He stepped back and sat on the edge of the bed, leaving a little space between them. Not retreating and not advancing either.

"I don't like how that came out," he said, more softly. "I'm worried about you and I don't know how to say that without sounding angry." The words surprised him as he spoke them, as they were not planned and they felt exposed.

There was a long pause. Amir did not respond straight away.

The tapping foot slowed, then stopped. The headphones remained on, but the music had gone quiet.

"I don't want you worrying about me all the time," Amir said eventually, still not looking up. "It makes everything feel like a test."

Something in Farid loosened then. Not relief, more like grief. A recognition of how his care had begun to feel like pressure and how his efforts to stay close had made the space tighter rather than safer.

They did not resolve anything that evening. The conversation drifted, stalled and circled back on itself. There were silences that felt awkward and others that felt oddly companionable. Eventually, Farid stood and left the room, not in frustration this time, just tired.

Later that night, lying awake, he replayed the moment in the hallway. The sound of the door, the surge of feeling and the urge to step in, to take control and to restore order. He could see the pattern more clearly now - how quickly fear had turned into firmness and how easily love had reached for authority when it felt threatened.

Nothing about that pattern felt unique to parenting. It was

the same movement he recognised elsewhere in his life. When someone he cared about pulled away. When uncertainty grew and the stakes felt too high to tolerate mess. Control was not the problem, control was the signal. It pointed to what he was trying to protect. The relationship, the hope of staying connected as things changed and the fear of becoming irrelevant in a life that was no longer organised around him. Over time, he learned to notice that signal earlier - the tightening in the chest, the impulse to intervene and the moment love began to sound like a command - not to eliminate it, just to recognise what it was guarding.

You might recognise this too. The moment you feel yourself bracing, moving to take charge and when care begins to feel like pressure. You might stay with that moment a little longer, long enough to sense what matters beneath it and long enough to meet the fear before it hardens into control.

There is no resolution here, just a widening of the space and sometimes that is enough.

Five:

Love That Refuses Rescue

Staying present without saving

The call came in the late afternoon, at that hour when the light begins to thin and the day feels as though it might finally loosen its grip. Anna recognised the tone of Claire's voice before the words arrived. Steady, measured, as if each sentence had been carefully selected and tested before being spoken aloud.

"I got the results today," Claire said. "It's not good." There was a pause after that. Not empty, but weighted, as though the words themselves needed time to settle into the space between them.

Terminal cancer is not something the body knows how to receive all at once. Anna felt it as a tightening in her chest, a quickening of breath and a sudden narrowing of attention. Her mind reached instinctively for questions. What did the doctors say? What were the options? What came next?

Claire spoke again. "I don't know what to do with this. It feels like the ground just disappeared."

"I'm here," Anna said quietly. "I'm with you."

They stayed on the line for a while after that, neither of them saying very much. The silence felt dense, almost tangible, but not awkward. Anna noticed how hard it was not to fill it, how strong the urge was to do something, to offer something and to be useful in a way that might ease the weight of what had just been named.

In the days that followed, that urge grew. It showed up late at night as searching for clinical trials, treatment protocols and stories of people who had lived longer than expected. Each one offered a small flare of hope, bright and fragile, like something that might burn out if held too tightly.

It showed up as optimism offered a little too quickly. "You're strong." "Medicine has come a long way." "You never know." It showed up as busyness with meals planned, routines adjusted and appointments offered to attend. Practicalities gathered and organised, as if activity itself could hold the fear at bay. All of it came from love.

And all of it, Anna slowly realised, risked making the space smaller.

She began to notice how her presence shifted when she was

trying to rescue, her listening became selective, gravitating toward anything that sounded hopeful and how she flinched, almost imperceptibly, when Claire spoke about fear or anger or the possibility of dying.

Rescue has a particular quality to it. It moves quickly, smooths edges and looks for exits.

One afternoon, they sat together by the window in Claire's living room. The light outside was pale and steady. A tree across the street moved gently in the breeze, its leaves making a soft, repetitive sound.

"I'm scared," Claire said, without drama or preamble. Just a simple statement, offered into the room.

Anna felt the familiar pull rise in her body. The urge to counter fear with reassurance. To remind Claire of what was still possible. To reach for something that might make the moment easier to bear. She noticed the pull and stayed.

"I know," she said. "I would be too." The words landed and stayed.

Claire's eyes filled then, slowly, not with panic, but with grief that had been waiting for permission. Anna stayed where she was, not reaching for tissues straight away and not speaking. She let the tears arrive in their own time. They sat like that for a long while. No plan. No reframing. No attempt to make meaning.

This was love refusing rescue, not because rescue was unkind, but because it was premature. Because it would have asked Claire to move away from what she was actually living.

Over the weeks that followed, this became a way of being together. When Claire spoke about fear, Anna stayed with fear. When anger surfaced, it was not redirected or softened. When the future was mentioned, it was allowed to remain uncertain.

There were moments when this felt almost unbearable. Moments when Anna went home and cried alone, the weight of what could not be changed pressing hard against her chest. Rescue would have been easier. Rescue would have allowed her to feel active, competent and useful, but it would also have taken something from Claire; the chance to speak honestly, to grieve without being managed and to remain herself, even as her life was changing irrevocably.

One evening, after a long visit in which very little had been said, Claire walked Anna to the door.

"Thank you," she said, almost casually, "for not trying to make this better."

Anna nodded, unable to reply immediately. She understood then that presence was not passive. It was not resignation. It required restraint, courage and a willingness to sit with helplessness without turning away.

Love that refuses rescue does not abandon hope. It simply does not demand it. It stays when there is nothing to do, listens when there is nothing to fix and remains when leaving would be easier. This kind of love often goes unnoticed as it leaves no visible trace, no story of triumph and no evidence of having helped. And yet, it changes the quality of the space in which suffering is lived.

You might recognise the pull to rescue in yourself, the moment silence feels intolerable, you reach for reassurance because fear is too close and you want to make it better, so you don't have to feel it. You might stay there for a breath longer than usual, not to do nothing forever, just long enough to let the other remain fully themselves.

Sometimes that is the only gift that can be given and sometimes, it is enough.

Collection II — Moments at the Edge

There is a place where the words line up and don't wait

where the answer is ready

and the room leans forward

it would be easy here

to call it clarity

to give it a name

and let the moment close

but something hesitates

not loudly

just enough to be felt

a hand not raised

a breath half taken

a pause with weight

a sentence unfinished

nothing breaks

nothing resolves

nothing is asked to leave

and still

the moment passes

having asked

Stephen Duns

what it came to ask

can we stay close to that place

not to decide

not too perfect

only to notice

what loosens

and what closes

when we do?

Stephen Duns

The chapters that follow are not examples of good leadership or wise living.

They are moments.

Moments when pressure rises and attention narrows. When responsibility weighs heavily. When love and power drift apart or find their way back into a relationship. Moments when something in the room or the family or the self, leans toward closure and something else quietly asks to be held.

Some of these moments soften. Others do not.

Nothing here is resolved neatly. There are no takeaways to

apply and no arc of improvement to admire. These stories are offered as places to pause, to recognise yourself, to notice what happens in you as you read. You don't need to agree with the choices made. You don't need to judge them either.

Let the stories work on you at their own pace, let them stir memory, resistance, recognition and let them leave questions unanswered.

Grace, when it appears, does so briefly. Grace, when it does not, leaves a trace.

This collection is an invitation to stay long enough to feel the difference.

Six:

When Control Isn't Working

Letting go without stepping away

He had never thought of himself as someone who clung to power. He would have said he carried responsibility, he made decisions when others hesitated and he kept things moving. He was proud of that. Not in a showy way, but in the quiet way a person becomes proud of what has kept them safe and useful for decades.

Gareth was in his late fifties now, a CEO who had come up through a world that rewarded certainty, speed and a particular kind of presence. He knew how to walk into a room and have it settle, how to end a debate and how to take the heat.

And if he was honest, he also knew how much the system had been built for someone like him. White, straight, male. Not because he had asked for it, but because it had been the air he breathed. He had not noticed it for a long time. Not really, you rarely notice privilege when it arrives as normal.

Lately, normal had been changing.

It was visible in the organisation, in the language people used and in the expectations that were shifting under his feet. There were new leaders in the room now, younger, more diverse, less willing to defer and more willing to name what had been unnamed. He told himself he supported it and he did, in principle. He had approved strategies, signed off on targets and spoken publicly about inclusion. He had done what he believed a decent leader should do in the times he was living in.

And still, inside him, something kept tightening. It wasn't hatred. It wasn't even opposition. It was resentment.

Not the loud kind, but the quiet, sour kind that surprised him when he noticed it. A feeling that he was being judged for an era he had not created. A feeling that the rules had changed and he was expected to apologise for succeeding within the old ones. A feeling that he was now meant to step back, make space, stay silent and be careful. As if his competence had become suspect simply because of who he was. He did not like that feeling as it didn't match his self-image or the way he wanted to see himself in the world.

So he managed it the way he managed most uncomfortable things. He worked harder.

The weeks leading up to the meeting had been relentless. Volume and pace, too many threads, too many competing priorities and too many signals, board expectations, media risk and staff fatigue. A complex change program that kept throwing up second-order consequences. He was sleeping, but not deeply. Eating, but without noticing. Moving through the days with a narrow kind of focus that he mistook for discipline.

Overload has a particular feel in the body. It isn't always dramatic, it can be quiet. A sense of being internally crowded, subtle irritability and shortened tolerance for nuance. The mind starts reaching for relief and relief looks like closure.

By the time Gareth walked into the executive meeting, he was already braced. He could feel it in the way his shoulders sat slightly higher than usual, in the way his jaw was set, in the way he wanted the conversation to move cleanly from point to point. He wanted progress, decisions and the mess reduced to something manageable.

The agenda was full and the first items went quickly. He kept things moving with familiar efficiency. Questions were answered. Options narrowed. Commitments secured.

People nodded, typed notes, followed his lead.

It looked like leadership.

Then the conversation shifted to the piece he had been dreading, though he would not have used that word. A proposal to change how senior roles were appointed. Not just the composition of panels, but the criteria, the pathways and the assumptions about what leadership looked like. There was a plan on the table, shaped by the diversity and inclusion lead and supported by several of his executives. It was not radical, not really. But it was different enough to disturb the old grooves. It asked for a redistribution of voice and influence in ways he could feel in his bones.

The Diversity and Inclusion lead, Leilani, a woman in her thirties, spoke calmly. She didn't posture, she didn't accuse, she explained the current patterns, the gaps, the costs and she spoke about capability and systems. She made space for others to contribute, was measured, thoughtful and clear.

Gareth listened and something in him tightened further. He noticed himself scanning for flaws. He noticed the impulse to challenge small details, to demand more data and to slow the proposal down. He could feel the familiar move toward certainty, the desire to narrow complexity into something he could control.

He could also feel the heat of something more personal, a thought he didn't want to have. So what, I'm the problem now? It wasn't said, but it was there.

He felt the pull toward a decisive response, something that would restore order and something that would put him back in familiar territory. He could hear his own voice already, confident and reasonable, drawing a line. Not shutting it down completely, just tightening the scope, delaying the timeline and placing it under review.

His executives were watching him. Not anxiously, exactly, more carefully. As if the room knew this was a hinge moment, even if no one named it.

He was aware of his authority in a way he hadn't been earlier in the meeting. The weight of it, the way it shaped what others did and did not say and how easily his mood could contract the room.

Someone spoke, offering a perspective about talent pipelines and the way informal sponsorship worked. Another added a story about a high-performing leader leaving because they couldn't see a future. The conversation began to widen, becoming more textured, more human. It was moving toward nuance.

Gareth felt impatience flare. This is going nowhere. We need a decision. That's what overload does. It makes texture feel like delay, complexity feel like threat, the mind craves clean lines and quick answers and certainty feels like safety.

He cleared his throat, preparing to speak. Then something small happened, almost invisible, not in the room, but in him. A flicker of awareness, recognition that his urge to control was not coming from wisdom or clarity, it was coming from strain, fatigue and a protective reflex that had served him well in a different era, but was now doing something else.

He noticed the resentment, not as a moral failure, but as a sensation. A tightening, a heat and a desire to reassert himself. He could feel how easy it would be to turn that sensation into policy, to convert discomfort into a decision that looked rational.

He stayed still for a moment longer than usual. The silence was not dramatic. No one would have called it profound. It was simply a pause in which he did not immediately reach for his usual tools.

In that pause, another feeling rose underneath the resentment.

Loss.

A quiet grief for a world in which he had been unquestioned, for a set of rules he understood and for a kind of authority that had felt clean and uncomplicated. He did not admire that world, not entirely, but it had been his home. He felt something soften, not in his opinions, but in his body. His shoulders lowered slightly. His breath widened. The urgency eased a fraction.

He spoke, but not in the way he had planned. "I can feel myself wanting to shut this down," he said, quietly, more to the room than to any one person. "Not because I think it's wrong. Because I'm overloaded and I'm reacting to what feels like more complexity."

The room changed, not with applause or relief, but with a subtle shift in attention. People leaned in. Someone's face softened. Leilani held his gaze for a moment, steady and not triumphant.

Gareth continued. "I also notice something else in me. A resentment I don't love. It's like a part of me is lamenting the loss of the old order, even though I know the old order wasn't fair. I don't want that part driving our decisions."

No one interrupted, no one rushed to reassure him and the space held. A different kind of conversation began then. Slower. More alive.

People spoke more truthfully, not only about the organisation, but about themselves. One executive admitted they had been afraid to name how much they were carrying. Another said they often moderated their tone in meetings like this, deciding in advance what would be safe to say. Someone else named that the change was not only structural but personal and that it brought up grief and defensiveness for many people, not just him.

Gareth listened and for the first time in weeks, he felt the system breathe. Responsibility began to be redistributed, not as abandonment of his role, but as a widening of ownership. The conversation was no longer a referendum on his identity, it was a shared attempt to hold a more complex truth.

The proposal did not become perfect. It did not become

simple. It remained messy in the way real shifts remain messy. There were still questions about timing, about capability, about unintended consequences.

But nuance was allowed to stay in the room.

He found himself asking different questions than he usually asked when under pressure. Not the questions that narrowed, but the questions that opened.

What would make this safe enough to try?

Where are we afraid and what are we protecting?

What do we need to learn as we go?

These were not soft questions. They were strong in a different way. Strong because they did not pretend the organisation could bypass discomfort. Strong because they invited honesty without forcing it.

A decision was still made, but it was not forced. It had the feel of something held rather than imposed. A pilot, a timeline, a commitment to review, a clear statement of intent. Enough structure to move, enough openness to learn.

When the meeting ended, Gareth did not feel triumphant. He felt tired, but not depleted. There was relief, but it was not the relief of closing things down. It was the relief of not having to carry the whole burden alone and not having to pretend he was untroubled. Later, walking to his car, he noticed how different the tiredness felt. Less brittle, less lonely. The kind that comes from staying present to complexity rather than escaping into certainty.

He knew the resentment would return at times. He was not cured of it. He knew overload would still happen. He knew contraction would still tempt him. These patterns had been shaped over a lifetime. But something had shifted. Power and love had re-entered the relationship, authority had settled rather than tightened and the system had been contained without being controlled.

And for a brief moment, something visited the room - Not a solution, not a moral victory and not an ending. Just a softening that made it possible for truth to be spoken and for responsibility to be shared.

You might recognise this moment, even if your context is different. The urge to simplify when you are overloaded, the tightening that feels like leadership, the resentment that surprises you or the pause that gives you back your choice. If you stay with that pause, even briefly, you might find that letting go does not require stepping away.

Sometimes it is simply the decision to loosen your grip enough for the room to breathe.

Seven:

When Certainty Cracks

Doubt as a doorway to deeper clarity

Priya had been certain going into the meeting. Not arrogantly or loudly so, just certain enough to feel steady in her own skin.

Priya had spent weeks making the decision. She was a woman in her early forties, a senior leader who had learned to respect complexity without being paralysed by it. She had done the work in the ways she trusted. The analysis had been thorough. Advice had been sought, including from people who were not inclined to agree with her. The plan made sense - it was defensible, well-reasoned and, importantly, it offered relief from a long period of ambiguity.

People had been asking for direction. This was direction.

As the meeting began, Priya spoke clearly and with confidence. The logic unfolded cleanly and the rationale was sound. Heads nodded, notes were taken and a few people typed as she spoke, the quiet clack of keys giving the room an air of productivity.

From the outside, it looked like alignment. Inside, something else was stirring.

Halfway through the explanation, Priya noticed a flicker of doubt. Not about the facts, but about the way the room was holding them. The nods felt polite, the silence felt careful and questions, when they came, stayed on the surface. A few faces held a neutrality that did not quite match the words being written down.

The doubt was quiet and easy to dismiss. This is just change fatigue, Priya thought. People will come around. She continued.

As the discussion opened, one person raised a concern. Hassan, a man in his thirties, was careful with his language, respected for how he did not make drama. His concern was framed gently, almost apologetically. A question about timing, a comment about readiness. He did not challenge the plan, he hovered near the edges of it, as if testing whether the room could tolerate a different tempo.

Priya answered competently and moved on.

Another person hesitated before speaking. Mei, a woman in her late twenties, newer to the senior group, conscientious, sometimes overly so. "I'm probably overthinking this," she said, then named a risk that had already been considered and ruled out.

Priya felt irritation rise, quickly followed by resolve.

We've done this work, she thought. We can't reopen everything. She responded firmly, not harshly, but conclusively. The kind of response that closes a door without slamming it, sounds reasonable, even kind and yet leaves no room for the conversation to change the decision.

The room adjusted. People stopped offering half-formed thoughts. The energy shifted from exploration to execution. Chairs seemed to settle and pens moved faster. The questions became practical and narrow: What do we tell people? When do we start? Who owns which part? What are the comms lines?

Priya felt a sense of relief, the discomfort eased and the meeting moved efficiently toward closure. The decision was made.

Afterwards, walking back to her office, Priya felt something like satisfaction. The meeting had been orderly, no one had resisted and no one had derailed them. In a season where every part of the organisation felt stretched, it was almost a gift to have ninety minutes conclude with a clear outcome.

And yet, in the days that followed, the unease returned. Not as a clear regret, not as panic. More as a dull question that surfaced at odd moments. In the shower, on a walk and late at night when the house was quiet and her mind stopped being useful.

What was it they hadn't said? It was hard to locate. There was no single sentence she could point to. No obvious conflict. It was more like a faint itch beneath the skin, the sense that something had been present in the room and then quietly removed, like a chair being taken away without anyone announcing it.

Implementation began and resistance appeared in quieter forms. Deadlines slipped, enthusiasm was uneven, meetings were attended but not fully inhabited and conversations happened elsewhere. People complied in the room and then carried their real doubts into the corridor, into side chats or into carefully phrased emails sent late at night.

Priya found herself explaining the decision again and again, each time more carefully. She adjusted her tone, added context, clarified what she thought had been clear and listened for the question underneath the question. Certainty began to thin.

Weeks later, a conversation with a trusted colleague landed differently. Not confrontational, just honest. It was **Salma**, a woman Priya had worked with for years, someone who had a way of saying uncomfortable things without making them weapons. They were walking back from a site visit, coffee cups cooling in their hands, the kind of moment where the body is moving and the guard drops a little.

"I think people didn't disagree because they didn't feel invited to," Salma said. "It felt decided before the conversation started."

The words stayed.

Priya didn't argue. She didn't defend herself. She felt the sentence land and lodge, not as an accusation, but as something she could not unseen. That evening, she replayed the meeting in her mind.

The flicker of doubt, the polite nods, the careful silence, Hassan's gentle concern, Mei's hesitation and her own irritation. The tightening in her chest that she had barely noticed at the time. The move to close things down. Nothing dramatic had gone wrong. There had been no blow-up. No obvious mistake. Just a moment where certainty had overridden curiosity. Where the desire for clarity had crowded out listening. Where she had unknowingly taught the room that the safest contribution was agreement.

This is how certainty cracks.

Not in the meeting itself, but later. When the system resists what it was not allowed to influence. When confidence gives way to second-guessing. When the cost of moving too quickly becomes visible over time, in a hundred small frictions rather than one loud failure.

Doubt, in these moments, is not a failure of leadership. It is information that arrived too quietly to be heard when it first appeared.

Sometimes certainty needs to hold, decisions must be made and action must follow. But sometimes certainty is defending us from something more uncomfortable than not knowing. From the vulnerability of staying open a little longer, from the risk of being changed by what we might hear and from the possibility that the plan is not wrong, but incomplete and that incompleteness asks for relationship, not just logic.

Priya did not reverse the decision. She lived with it. She adjusted where she could. She widened the consultation on the next phases. She invited Hassan and Mei into a smaller conversation, not to revisit the past, but to understand what they had felt in that room. She noticed how often she reached for certainty when discomfort arose, how quickly she translated unease into closure.

The next time doubt appeared, it was recognised sooner. Not resolved. Just noticed.

You might recognise this moment. The subtle doubt you brushed past, the relief of closing things down or the uncertainty that returned later, asking to be met.

There is nothing here to correct. Just something to remember. Sometimes doubt is not a problem to eliminate, it is a doorway we didn't step through.

Eight:

When Conflict Holds More Than Threat

Staying in disagreement without collapse

Daniel had been rehearsing the conversation for weeks, though he wouldn't have described it that way. It lived in him as a low-level hum, a background tension that followed him through ordinary days. While cooking dinner, while walking to work or while lying awake beside Michael, listening to the quiet rhythm of another body in the dark.

It wasn't that he didn't know what he wanted to say. That part was clear enough. What he didn't know was whether saying it would cost him something he wasn't ready to lose.

His family had always been religious. Not casually so. Faith shaped the rhythms of their lives, the language they used to make sense of the world and the way love and belonging were organised. Church every Sunday, prayer before meals and a shared moral grammar that had once felt unquestioned and secure.

When Daniel came out in his late twenties, the rupture wasn't explosive. No shouting, no dramatic scenes, just a slow withdrawal that was almost harder to name.

Conversations became careful, visits shorter and certain topics quietly disappeared. His parents continued to say they loved him, but they just couldn't accept this part of his life. For years, Daniel learned how to live inside that gap.

He compartmentalised. He didn't bring partners home or mention dates. He let his family imagine a version of his life that was partial and manageable. It was a form of peace, but it came at a cost - each omission shaved something off him and each accommodation asked him to be smaller.

Then he met Michael.

There was nothing dramatic about it. They met through friends, coffee turned into walks and walks into dinners. Time settled around them in a way that felt unforced. Michael had a steadiness Daniel hadn't known he was looking for, the capacity to stay present without pushing and to listen without disappearing into himself.

When they decided to get married, the joy arrived alongside something else. A reckoning.

Daniel knew what he wanted. He wanted his parents there not just in name, but in presence. He wanted Michael welcomed into the family, not tolerated at the edges. He wanted photographs that didn't need explaining away. A table where no one was pretending.

He also knew the risk. As the wedding plans began to take shape, the old anxiety returned with force. His chest felt tight more often than not. He caught himself scanning for signs of rejection before anything had been said. He felt the familiar pull to manage the situation, to soften the ask, to make it easier for them to say no.

Conflict, for Daniel, had always carried a threat. Not threat of violence or abandonment outright, but threat of withdrawal, silence and the quiet loss of connection.

The night before he planned to speak to them, he barely slept. His mind kept circling the same questions. How hard do I push? How much do I protect myself? What am I willing to lose? He noticed an old pattern waking up in him. The urge to choose clarity over relationship or relationship over truth. To frame the conversation in a way that would minimise discomfort, even if it meant erasing parts of himself.

That morning, he sat alone for a long time before picking up the phone. When his mother answered, her voice was warm, familiar. She asked about work, the weather and whether he was eating well. The ordinary kindness of it almost undid him.

Eventually, he told her about the wedding. The date, the place and the plans. There was a pause on the other end of the line. He felt his body brace, his shoulders lifted and his breath shortened.

"We don't know how to feel about this," she said carefully. "You know what we believe."

"Yes," Daniel said. "I do."

Another pause.

"I want you there," he continued, feeling his heart hammer. "Both of you. I want you to meet Michael properly. I want him welcomed into the family and I need to know whether that's possible." The words landed heavier than he had expected. Saying them out loud made the stakes unmistakable.

His mother didn't respond immediately. When she did, her voice sounded strained. "We love you," she said. "But this goes against everything we've been taught."

Daniel felt the familiar surge of anger rise, hot and fast. The urge to argue, to dismantle theology and to list the ways he had already compromised himself for their comfort. He also felt something else. A grief that had been there for years, now pressing close to the surface. Grief for the family he wanted but didn't quite have. Grief for how much energy it took to stay connected at all.

He took a breath. Not a deliberate one. Just the next one that came. "I'm not asking you to change your beliefs," he said slowly. "I'm asking you to stay in relationship with me without pretending that this part of my life doesn't exist."

The line was quiet. He could hear movement on the other end. The faint sound of someone shifting in a chair.

"This is very hard for us," his mother said.

"I know," Daniel replied. "It's hard for me too."

Something in the tone of the conversation shifted then. Not resolution, not agreement, but a subtle settling, as if the fight they had both been bracing for didn't arrive.

Over the weeks that followed, the conversation continued in fragments. A difficult phone call, an email sent and rewritten and long silences that carried more than absence.

There were moments when Daniel felt himself hardening. Times when he thought about withdrawing entirely, cutting his losses, protecting himself from further disappointment. There were other moments when he was tempted to collapse back into accommodation, to tell Michael they should just have a smaller ceremony, a quieter life.

Neither option felt true.

Staying in disagreement required something else. It required Daniel to hold his ground without turning it into a weapon. To remain open without begging and allow his parents their struggle without letting it erase him.

When they finally met Michael, it was awkward. Polite, stilted with no hugs or grand gestures. But they stayed and asked questions. They listened, even when they didn't know what to say.

At one point, his father said quietly, "This isn't easy for us."

Daniel nodded. "It isn't for me either."

The wedding came. His parents sat in the second row. Not at the front, not hidden away. They did not smile through the whole ceremony. They did not leave. Afterwards, his mother hugged him tightly. She did not hug Michael. But she did speak to him. She thanked him for loving her son.

It was not everything Daniel had hoped for and it was not nothing.

Conflict had not resolved itself. Beliefs had not suddenly aligned. Pain had not disappeared. But something had been held. The disagreement did not collapse into silence or explode into rupture. It stayed in the room, alive, unfinished and carried.

Over time, that mattered. Daniel learned that conflict is not always a sign that a relationship has failed. Sometimes it is the only place where a relationship can become more honest. Not because everyone agrees, but because no one disappears. Staying did not mean enduring anything. It meant staying present to himself as well as to them. It meant refusing to trade truth for belonging or belonging for truth.

You might recognise this edge. The moment disagreement threatens the connection. The urge to win or withdraw, the fear that standing your ground will cost you everything. You might notice what happens if you stay just where you are, not forcing resolution and not abandoning yourself.

Sometimes conflict holds more than a threat. Sometimes it holds the possibility of a relationship that is narrower than you wished, but truer than what came before. And sometimes, staying is the bravest thing love can do.

Nine:

Radical Candour and Radical Tenderness

A feedback conversation where truth can either wound or heal

Version one: Candour without tenderness and the clean cut that leaves a scar

The conversation had been booked for thirty minutes and, on paper, it was nothing unusual. Just a regular one-on-one that had finally been upgraded in Amina's mind to something more serious, because there were patterns that had stopped being annoying and had started becoming costly.

Amina was the General Manager of a fast moving service team, a woman who had earned her authority in the kind of environments where you are either clear or you are swallowed. She had developed a reputation for being fair, sharp and reliable, which meant that when she spoke, people often listened and when she made a call, it tended to hold.

The person she was meeting with was Rafi, a man in his early thirties, clever and charismatic in a way that could lift a room when it landed well and derail it when it didn't. In recent months his work had developed a faint shimmer of inconsistency, not obvious enough to be a performance issue on any single day, but cumulative enough that others were covering for him and then resenting him and then going quiet around him. Amina could feel the system beginning to organise itself around the avoidance.

She had delayed this conversation twice, not because she didn't know what to say, but because she knew exactly what she wanted to say and she could feel the force of it. In the middle of a crowded week the force had started to look like efficiency and efficiency, she told herself, would be kind in its own way, because dragging things out was cruel.

On the morning of the meeting, she moved fast, too fast and not only in her calendar. She moved fast inside herself as well. She skimmed her notes while walking, she answered three emails she should have ignored, she drank coffee that tasted like urgency and by the time she sat down, she could feel her mind lining up the points like neat weapons laid out on a table, clean and justified and ready.

Rafi arrived two minutes late, smiling as if the clock was an amiable suggestion and not a boundary. He slid into the chair with a friendliness that might have been disarming if Amina had not already made herself armour.

"Thanks for making the time," he said and there was warmth in it and a hint of charm, as if the relationship itself could soften the matter at hand.

Amina nodded, looked down at her notes and went straight to the centre.

"This is a performance conversation," she said, calm and even. She watched his face change in a way he probably thought was subtle, but she had learned to read the micro shifts; the eyes that blinked once too long, the jaw that set and the smile that stayed on but no longer reached the skin around the eyes.

She kept going.

"I'm going to be direct. Your follow-through has been inconsistent. Deadlines are being missed, quality is uneven and the impact is that other people are carrying your load or cleaning up after you. It's not sustainable and it's not acceptable."

The words were accurate. That was the problem and the comfort. They were accurate enough to feel like righteousness.

Rafi opened his mouth, then closed it. Amina interpreted that as the usual move, the beginning of explanation, of story, of reasons that would make sense individually and would still leave the pattern intact and her impatience rose like a hand already reaching for the door handle to end the conversation.

"I'm not looking for explanations," she added, not harshly, but with a finality that took the air out of the room. "I'm looking for a change and I'm looking for it now."

Rafi's shoulders tightened and because he was intelligent and proud, his intelligence began to defend him before his heart had even caught up.

"That's not really fair," he said and there was a flash of heat under the politeness. "I've been carrying a lot and I've delivered on plenty and I'm not the only one who's been slipping."

Amina felt the familiar surge. The part of her that had learned, long ago, that the fastest way through conflict is to become more certain.

"This isn't a comparison," she said. "This is about you and

I'm telling you what I'm seeing."

She leaned forward slightly as she spoke, not dramatically, but enough. Her voice stayed controlled, which made the firmness feel even more absolute, because there was no messiness to soften it, no human friction to signal that she was still with him and not simply over him.

Rafi stared at the table for a moment and when he looked up his eyes were brighter, not with tears but with the kind of anger that tries to stay contained so it can still appear reasonable.

"So what do you want?" he asked.

Amina listed actions. They were sensible actions; weekly check-ins, clear deliverables and a reallocation of responsibilities until trust was rebuilt. A documented performance plan was used if improvement was not evident quickly. She spoke like someone who could solve anything, because competence had been her refuge for years and right now she was hiding in it as if it were a fortress.

Rafi nodded at the right points. He agreed with the words. He even repeated back the commitments in a way that sounded mature.

But something in him had already stepped back.

Amina could feel it, even as she ticked the final box. The atmosphere had shifted from relationship to transaction. She told herself that this was what professionalism required and yet a quieter part of her knew that what had just happened was not clean clarity, it was a clean cut.

The meeting ended on time.

Rafi left with a polite thank you and a steady gait and only after the door closed did Amina notice her own body. The held breath, the tension in her shoulders, the faint buzzing under her skin as if she had just pushed through a storm without getting wet and she felt a small, immediate relief.

For the next week, the surface improved.

Rafi's work became punctual. Emails were crisp. Tasks were delivered. Meetings were attended with a new seriousness. On paper, it looked like progress.

And yet the team's energy did not lift. It dulled.

People stopped asking Rafi for input unless they had to. He stopped offering ideas unless invited. He became quieter and more compliant, less alive. His work met the brief, but it no longer carried any of him and the system, which had wanted accountability, now found itself missing something it hadn't realised it relied on, a kind of engagement that cannot be coerced.

Amina began to sense the consequence, not as an obvious failure but as a thinning and she caught herself feeling irritated at his new politeness, which was its own kind of accusation.

One afternoon, she overheard two team members speaking in the kitchen. They lowered their voices when she walked in, then smiled too brightly. She felt the old familiar sting, the knowledge that the room had reorganised around caution and she was now part of the reason.

She went back to her office and stared at her calendar and she found herself thinking, not with pride, not with regret, but with a kind of quiet discomfort that had no easy home.

I told the truth, she thought.

Yes.

And something is still closed.

Version two: Candour with tenderness and the pause that makes room for grace to visit

The conversation had been booked for thirty minutes and, on paper, it was nothing unusual. Just a regular one-on-one that had finally been upgraded in Amina's mind to something more serious, because there were patterns that had stopped being annoying and had started becoming costly.

Amina was the General Manager of a fast moving service team, a woman who had earned her authority in the kind of environments where you are either clear or you are swallowed. She had developed a reputation for being fair, sharp and reliable, which meant that when she spoke, people often listened and when she made a call, it tended to hold.

The person she was meeting with was Rafi, a man in his early thirties, clever and charismatic in a way that could lift a room when it landed well and derail it when it didn't. In recent months his work had developed a faint shimmer of inconsistency, not obvious enough to be a performance issue on any single day, but cumulative enough that others were covering for him, then resenting him and then going quiet around him and Amina could feel the system beginning to organise itself around the avoidance.

She had delayed this conversation twice, not because she didn't know what to say, but because she knew exactly what she wanted to say and she could feel the force of it. She had begun to notice something else as well, a small and stubborn part of her that wanted this to be clean and decisive, partly because she was tired and partly because she liked the feeling of being the one who could land the plane when everyone else was circling. That recognition did not make her weak. It made her more honest.

On the morning of the meeting, she still moved quickly, because that was the week she was in and the system did not pause to accommodate her inner work, but she did one small thing differently. Before Rafi arrived, she put her notes face down on the table and let herself feel the truth of what she was carrying, which was not only frustration, but responsibility and care and a faint grief that this conversation was necessary at all. She had once liked Rafi's spark and had enjoyed his liveliness in the team and now she was about to risk that relationship in order to protect something larger.

Rafi arrived two minutes late, smiling as if the clock was an amiable suggestion and not a boundary. He slid into the chair with a friendliness that might have been disarming if Amina had not been paying attention.

"Thanks for making the time," he said and there was warmth in it and a hint of charm, as if the relationship itself could soften the matter at hand.

Amina nodded and this time she did not look down at her notes straight away, because she wanted to meet him first as a person and not as a problem.

"I need to talk about something that matters," she said. "And I'm going to be direct, but I also want to do it in a way that keeps us in relationship, because I don't want to win a point and lose the trust between us."

Rafi blinked and, for a moment, his smile faltered into something more vulnerable, as if he had been expecting attack or avoidance and had received neither and his ego, which had been ready to defend, hesitated.

Amina continued.

"I've noticed a pattern of inconsistency in your follow-through. Deadlines are being missed, quality is uneven and the impact is that other people are carrying your load or cleaning up after you. It's not sustainable, it's not fair on them and it's also not fair on you, because it is putting you in a position where people are losing confidence and you might not even fully know it's happening."

The words were still accurate. The truth was not diluted. But the tone carried something else. Not softness as avoidance, but tenderness as contact.

Rafi looked down at the table and Amina could see his shoulders tighten and she felt, in her own body, the familiar impulses start to stir. The impulse to reassure, which would be a rescue. The impulse to push, which would be a blade. She noticed both and because she noticed them, she had a third option, which was to slow down.

"I'm watching this land," she said quietly. "And I can imagine it might feel like a lot. Before we go into what needs to change, I want to ask, what's happening in you as you hear this?"

There was a pause and it was not comfortable, because real tenderness rarely is, at least not at first. Rafi's mind scrambled for the familiar exits, humour, defensiveness, explanation and then something in him seemed to tire of his own performance.

"I feel embarrassed," he said and the word surprised him, you could tell by the way it came out, slightly rough, as if it had been pulled up from a place he didn't usually show. "And I feel angry, because I've been trying and I also feel… I don't know. Like I'm letting everyone down."

Amina felt the room change, not dramatically, but like a window opening a crack in a stuffy house. She noticed how quickly her own heart softened and how quickly her mind wanted to take advantage of that softening by making the conversation lighter and easier, less consequential. She resisted that. Tenderness without candour would be its own betrayal.

"Thank you for saying that," she said. "And I'm going to stay with the truth as well, because the impact is real. I need you to take responsibility for what's happening and I also don't want you to carry it as shame, because shame will either make you defensive or make you disappear and neither helps you or the team."

Rafi swallowed. He nodded, once, not the nod of compliance but the nod of someone recognising a line they can no longer step around.

He started to explain, as people do and some of what he

said mattered and some of it was a familiar story. Amina listened differently than she had planned, not because she was letting him off the hook, but because she was more interested in what was true than what was tidy.

In the middle of his explanation, he said something small, almost accidental.

"I keep telling myself I can catch up," he said and then gave a short laugh that had no humour in it, only fatigue. "I keep thinking if I just push harder, no one will notice."

Amina could have pounced on that. She could have turned it into a lesson or a diagnosis or a neat insight. Instead, she let it sit.

"Yes," she said and she let the word carry recognition rather than judgment. "I think I can see that."

They talked about the practicalities, because practicality matters and love without power becomes a fog and Amina was not offering fog. She was offering a way forward that protected the team and protected Rafi's chance to recover his integrity.

They agreed on clear deliverables. They agreed on weekly check-ins. They agreed on what would happen if things did not improve. But woven through the actions was something else and it was not sentimental. It was simply the sense that Amina was not asking for performance, she was asking for responsibility and she was not withholding dignity while she asked.

At one point, Rafi said, "So you're saying I've been dropping the ball and you're also saying you're not done with me."

Amina exhaled and she could feel, again, how thin the line was.

"Yes," she said. "That's exactly what I'm saying."

The meeting ended, not with relief, not with triumph, but with a kind of quiet steadiness, as if they had both survived something real without needing to turn it into drama. In the next week, the surface improved, just as it had in the first version. Deadlines were met, emails were crisp and tasks were delivered. But this time the team's energy shifted differently. Not instantly and not perfectly, but in small ways that were almost easy to miss unless you were watching for them.

Rafi asked for help before he drowned. He admitted, once, in a meeting, that he had overcommitted and instead of making a joke, he paused and let the admission stand, which was brave in its own quiet way. Someone else nodded, as if grateful that the room could hold that kind of truth without turning it into theatre.

Amina noticed that people began approaching Rafi again with small questions and early drafts and he responded with something like himself, not the old swagger, but a steadier presence that did not need to impress anyone to be useful.

It was not a perfect arc. There were slips. There were days when Rafi fell into old habits and days when Amina's patience shortened and she could feel herself wanting to tighten the screws. But they had established something that made those moments workable.

The truth could be spoken without being weaponised.

Care could be offered without becoming a rescue.

In the middle of it, almost invisibly, grace visited, not as a glowing experience, but as a small easing in the field, as if everyone's shoulders dropped a fraction and the air moved again.

Amina would not have called it a breakthrough. She would have called it a conversation. But later, when she thought back on it, she could see the hinge.

The same facts.

The same performance issue.

The same need for change.

And one small difference, a pause where she chose contact before control and truth before comfort and then held both long enough for something in the relationship to stay intact.

You might recognise both versions, perhaps even in yourself, because most of us have spoken hard truths and most of us have tried to soften hard moments. The question is not whether candour or tenderness is better, but what happens when they are forced to share the same room.

If you are reading this and feeling your own body respond, perhaps tightening at the thought of giving feedback or softening at the thought of receiving it, you might simply stay with that sensation for a moment longer than usual, not to fix it and not to make a plan, but to notice what it is protecting and what it is costing.

Sometimes the difference between a clean cut and a living conversation is not the words. It is the inner place the words come from and whether there was room, even briefly, for a glisk.

Ten:

When the System Leans on You

Being offered what the whole cannot hold

It didn't arrive all at once.

The exhaustion had been in the system long before it found me. It lived in the pace of the work, in the accumulation of unfinished change and in the sense that everyone was carrying more than they could name. It showed up in small ways at first, a sharper edge in conversations, weariness behind people's eyes and the quiet relief when someone else took responsibility.

By the time I stepped into the CEO role, the organisation was already tired. I could feel it almost immediately, not as a set of complaints or data points, but as an atmosphere. Meetings that felt heavier than their agendas suggested and decisions that took more energy than expected. People are working hard and still feeling behind.

At first, I responded the way I had learned to respond over many years. I listened, took things on and tried to absorb the pressure so others wouldn't have to. I stayed visible, available and steady.

This is how leadership often works when things are strained. The system looks for someone who can carry what it cannot. Someone with enough authority, enough composure and enough apparent capacity to hold the weight. I was good at that. I had been trained for it, shaped by it and rewarded for it. Being the one who could take the heat without flinching had become part of my identity long ago. It felt familiar, even necessary.

For a while, it worked;. people seemed relieved, conversations became more candid and long-held frustrations found a place to land. There was a sense that finally someone was listening, finally someone was taking responsibility. I noticed, though, that I was increasingly tired in a way that rest did not touch. Not the fatigue of long hours, but a deeper depletion. A sense of being saturated, as if the air around me was thick with something I couldn't quite name.

I began waking in the early hours of the morning, my mind already busy and my body tight. During the day, I caught myself feeling irritable in moments that didn't warrant it. I felt unusually reactive to small things. The edges of my patience thinned.

At first, I assumed it was just the intensity of the role, normal adjustment and something to push through, but the feeling persisted.

It was during a conversation with a trusted colleague that something shifted. They were speaking about the organisation's exhaustion, naming it openly for the first time. As I listened, I felt a familiar tightening in my gut, the same sensation that had been with me for weeks.

And then, unexpectedly, I noticed something else. The exhaustion didn't feel like mine. This wasn't an intellectual insight, it arrived in my body. A subtle but unmistakable distinction, as if the weight I had been carrying moved from inside me to just in front of me, where it could be seen rather than absorbed. I realised I had been holding the system's exhaustion as if it were a personal failing or limitation, as if my job was to metabolise it on behalf of everyone else.

That realisation changed the quality of my attention. I began to notice how often people brought their weariness, frustration and disappointment to me. Sometimes directly, sometimes indirectly, through tone, implication or expectation. I could feel how easily I stepped into the role of container, how readily I took responsibility for feelings that were not mine to resolve.

This is how systems lean. Not maliciously or consciously, they lean on whoever appears able to stand. The danger is not that the system leans. It is that the person being leaned on forgets to notice.

Once I saw it, I couldn't unsee it. I began to experiment, carefully. Not withdrawing, but shifting how I listened. When people spoke of exhaustion, I named it back to them without owning it. When frustration was directed at me, I acknowledged it without defending or fixing. When the impulse to reassure arose, I paused. Instead of absorbing the weight, I held it in the room, as an object for inquiry and reflection.

"It sounds like we are all carrying more than we've admitted," I would say or "There's a lot of tiredness here and I don't think it belongs to any one person."

At first, this unsettled people. Some looked relieved, others looked anxious and a few became frustrated. If I wasn't going to take it on, then where was it meant to go?

The system wobbled. Transparency has consequences.

When what has been held silently is named, it doesn't disappear, it spreads and asks to be shared.

Meetings became harder before they became more honest, conversations lengthened and emotions surfaced that had been carefully managed away. There were moments when it would have been easier to step back into the old pattern, to absorb the discomfort and smooth things over. I felt that pull acutely. There were days when I left work feeling exposed rather than competent. When the urge to retreat, to protect himself from the sheer volume of feeling, was strong, when I wondered if I had made things worse by opening the door.

This was the unintended consequence of presence. By not taking the exhaustion on, I had made it visible and visibility required work.

Gradually, something else began to happen. Responsibility started to redistribute, not evenly and not without resistance, but perceptibly. People began speaking to each other more directly. Teams started naming limits rather than quietly exceeding them. The organisation began to see itself more clearly, not as a collection of individual failures, but as a system under strain. The exhaustion didn't vanish.

It was still there. But it was no longer lodged in one body.

I noticed a difference in me, too. I was still tired, but the tiredness had changed. It no longer felt like erosion, it felt like effort. Like the honest cost of staying present to something difficult without collapsing into it. There were still days when the system leaned hard, when anxiety spiked and when people looked to me for certainty I would not offer.

I learned to notice those moments earlier; the tightening, the urge to reassure and the temptation to carry what wasn't mine. Sometimes I succeeded. Sometimes I didn't. But the distinction mattered. Being leaned on is not a failure of leadership. It is often a sign that the system senses someone who can hold complexity. The work is not to refuse the offer outright, it is to decide, moment by moment, what can be held and what must be returned to the whole.

This kind of leadership is not glamorous. It doesn't produce quick wins or clear narratives of success. There is always the seduction of rescuing, even being the messiah. It requires stamina, humility and a willingness to be misunderstood. It also requires trust. Trust that a system can learn to carry itself if given the chance and that naming reality, even when it destabilises, is a form of care.

You might recognise this moment. The point where you feel more tired than makes sense, the sense of being the place where everything lands or the quiet confusion about why rest doesn't restore you.

You might pause there, not to harden, not to withdraw but to ask what you have been holding that does not belong to you alone. Sometimes the most generous act is not to carry more, but to help the whole learn to hold what it has been avoiding.

And sometimes, that is where something begins to heal.

Eleven:

When the Human Comes First

Choosing presence over protocol

The first time it went wrong, it didn't look wrong at all.

The plan was solid, the governance was clear, the milestones were sensible and the language was reassuring. There were diagrams, timelines and risk registers that spoke the dialect of good change. From the outside, it had the calm confidence of something that had been done before and would be done again. People were consulted, briefings were held, questions were answered and decisions were made.

Still, something in the organisation began to strain. It showed up as compliance without commitment, meetings that felt technically productive and emotionally dead, people doing what was asked while quietly disengaging from why it mattered and as a growing sense of weariness that couldn't be traced to workload alone.

The process was working. The humans were not.

At the time, this was hard to name. It is much easier to see what is missing in hindsight. When you are inside it, process has a persuasive authority of its own. It promises order, fairness and protection from chaos and conflict. And when things feel fragile, that promise is seductive.

Francios leaned into it. He was a man in his early fifties, the kind of leader who had built his life on being dependable. He didn't seek attention, he sought traction. He didn't want to be admired, he wanted things to work. In his world, when people were anxious, clarity was kindness and when systems were messy, structure was care. He had been rewarded for that stance for a long time.

So he focused on getting the mechanics right, clarifying roles, tightening accountability and making sure the steps were followed in the right order, when resistance appeared, it was interpreted as a communication problem or a capability gap. Something to be managed.

The harder Francois pushed the process, the more brittle the system became. People stopped bringing their whole selves to the work. Conversations moved to the margins. Energy drained away in ways that spreadsheets could not capture. The organisation looked like it was changing, but underneath, something vital was being bypassed.

There were small signs he did not understand at first. The way people's faces went blank when the slides came up. The way the same questions kept being asked in different forms, as if the answer didn't quite land. The way the room became polite, not because everyone agreed, but because it felt safer to comply than to risk being seen as difficult. Even his own body began to signal it. A tightness in his throat before town halls and the urge to speak faster, to cover more ground, to reassure people by giving them more information. He mistook that urgency for responsibility.

What he learned, slowly and at some personal cost, was that process can move an organisation forward while leaving its people behind. That lesson stayed with him. So when Francois stepped into the next system, he carried a different question with him. Not "What is the right process?" but "What is this system living through?"

He could feel the fatigue early. The accumulation of unfinished change, the sense of fragmentation and the quiet mistrust that builds when people have adapted themselves too many times without feeling seen. It was in the way people spoke carefully, as if words had been used against them before. It was in the way managers carried a kind of brittle cheerfulness that didn't match their eyes. It was in the way staff meetings began with updates and ended with a silence that lingered too long.

There was pressure to move quickly, to stabilise and to reassure funders, boards and partners that things were under control. The familiar tools were ready at hand; project plans, structural redesigns and clear lines of accountability. Francois did not abandon them, but he refused to let them lead alone. Instead, he held two things in view at the same time. The need for structure and the need for human sense-making. The outer work of change and the inner work of adaptation. Process and person, moving together.

It felt riskier than he expected. Opening the system up to real conversation meant tolerating uncertainty. It meant inviting voices that would complicate the picture rather than simplify it. It meant hearing frustration that had nowhere to go before. It meant naming tensions that had been smoothed over in the past.

Not everyone welcomed this. Some wanted clarity, not conversation. Some worried that the work would stall. Some found the emotional exposure uncomfortable and unnecessary. There were moments when Francois wondered if he had misjudged the timing or overestimated the organisation's capacity. There were also moments when he could feel himself reaching for the old protection. The urge to retreat into the clean world of deliverables, where everything could be tracked, counted and reported. The itch to make the mess disappear by turning it into a plan.

But he stayed. He chose presence over protocol, again and again. He spent time listening without immediately converting what he heard into action items. He named what he was noticing in the room, even when it slowed things down. He acknowledged the cost of change alongside its necessity. He made space for people to speak from experience rather than position.

To support that, he began to work closely with Anjali, a woman in her late thirties who held a senior role in learning and development. She had a way of noticing what was happening beneath the words, the way a room could agree while still withholding itself. She was not interested in grand emotional displays. She was interested in what was real.

In meetings, when the conversation started to become

overly smooth, Anjali would sometimes ask something simple. "What are we not saying?" Or she would notice the energy shifting and name it with quiet accuracy. "I'm sensing a lot of agreement, and I'm not sure it's the same as alignment."

Francois began to value those interruptions, even when they made him uncomfortable. Especially then. Something shifted. Not quickly and not evenly, but perceptibly. Meetings became messier and more alive, disagreements surfaced earlier rather than later and people began speaking to each other rather than through hierarchy. The work felt harder in the short term and more coherent over time.

The process still mattered. Decisions were still made. Structures were still clarified. But they were shaped in conversation with the people who had to live inside them. The system was no longer being rearranged from above, it was learning from within.

There were unintended consequences. Some people found the openness confronting. Long-held grievances emerged that required attention and old loyalties were tested. The organisation wobbled as it learned to hold more truth than it had before. There were days when it felt as if the lid had been taken off a pot that had been simmering for years. The steam did not come out politely. It came out in bursts. Sharp questions, tired anger, tears that surprised the person who shed them and quiet exits from meetings when someone reached their limit.

This was the price of choosing the human first, and it was also the gift. Because alongside the disruption came something else. A sense of shared ownership, renewed willingness to engage and a feeling that people were not just being changed, but changing together.

Francois noticed it in small moments. A staff member naming a limit without apology. A leader admitting, they didn't have the answer. A team staying in a difficult conversation rather than rushing to closure. He noticed it in his own body, too. The difference between the tiredness that comes from pushing and the tiredness that comes from staying. Less brittle, less lonely and more honest.

The system began to breathe.

Looking back, he could see that the difference was not a better model or a smarter framework, though those helped. The difference was the decision to treat human development as integral rather than incidental. To recognise that no amount of technical excellence can substitute for the slow work of helping people adapt to what is being asked of them.

Process without presence had failed him before. Presence without process would have failed here too. What mattered was the relationship between them.

Choosing the human first did not mean abandoning rigour. It meant grounding rigour in reality, allowing structures to emerge in dialogue with lived experience and accepting that progress would sometimes look like disruption before it looked like alignment.

You might recognise this tension. The pull toward tidy plans when things feel fragile, the temptation to prioritise movement over meaning or the belief that if the process is right, the people will follow.

You might pause there and ask what would happen if, just for a moment, presence led and protocol followed?

Twelve:

When Grace Does Not Appear

Naming the moments that hardened

The Meeting That Ended on Time

The meeting began with the kind of energy people sometimes mistake for alignment. Everyone arrived on time, papers were read and the numbers were known. The options had been narrowed in pre-meetings and corridor conversations, so the room held a quiet sense of inevitability. Even the small talk felt controlled, purposeful, as if the system was conserving its remaining capacity for what mattered.

Khaled sat at the head of the table and felt, with a kind of tired relief, that today could be clean. There had been too many messy meetings recently, too many conversations that expanded into complexity and then ended without anything solid to hold. He had told himself that openness was good, consultation was necessary and nuance mattered, but he could feel the cost of it accumulating in his body. The late nights. The sense of being crowded internally. The tightening that arrived when another question opened another thread.

Overload had been building for months. Volume and pace, competing priorities, too many inputs and not enough quiet. Khaled had started to notice the way his thinking changed under that load. How quickly he moved toward closure. How impatient he became with questions that did not immediately translate into action. How tempting it was to mistake speed for decisiveness and decisiveness for safety.

He told himself he was being responsible. He was also, if he was honest, tired of holding uncertainty.

The agenda moved briskly, items were handled efficiently and a few careful jokes landed and faded. People spoke in the language of competence. Metrics, risks and mitigation. It all sounded reassuring. The room was orderly. Khaled's shoulders settled a fraction. It felt good to be in a place where things could be managed.

Then they reached the decision. It was not a trivial decision. It involved people, workload, change and reputation. There were trade-offs no one wanted to own. It had been circling for weeks. Khaled could feel the collective expectation gathering, the unspoken wish that he would simply land it so everyone could move on.

A senior manager raised a concern early, politely. Not challenging the decision itself, but more the timing. A soft question about capacity. Another asked about downstream consequences for a particular team, a question with more emotion in it than the words suggested.

Khaled heard the questions and felt a contraction. A narrowing of attention. A small heat behind the sternum. If we go down this path, we will be here all day.

He answered the first concern with crisp competence, referencing data, pointing to mitigations already in place. He acknowledged the second concern and offered reassurance that it would be managed through existing channels. He spoke clearly and calmly, he did not raise his voice and he did not dismiss anyone.

And yet something happened in the room. It was subtle, and that was part of the problem. When leaders harden under pressure, it does not always look like aggression. It can look like efficiency, sound like calm and be framed as professionalism.

But in the micro movements, the room began to thin.

People stopped offering half-formed thoughts, questions became safer and comments became shorter. Those who were uncertain decided, privately, that the uncertainty was not welcome here. The agenda marched on and Khaled felt a growing sense of control return, which felt like relief.

Someone at the far end of the table began to speak, then paused. Khaled noticed the pause and felt an urge to move on. They were behind time. He had another meeting straight after this. "It sounds like we are broadly aligned," he said, scanning for nods. There were nods.

That was the closing moment. Not dramatic or explicit. Just a small turning of the wheel that set everything on the new track.

The decision passed, actions were assigned and Khaled summarised the next steps and thanked everyone for their work. The meeting ended on time, people stood, gathered their papers and moved out into the corridor with the faintly brisk energy of people relieved to have something settled.

Khaled returned to his office and felt, for a few minutes, lighter. He had done what was needed. He had made the call. He had kept the system moving.

Then, over the next few days, a different feeling began to surface. It did not arrive as conflict, it arrived as drag. Teams did not resist openly, they complied. They asked questions that sounded technical, but the questions kept arriving. Clarifications, reclarifications and requests to revisit assumptions. A series of small obstacles that, taken individually, were reasonable, but taken together, they formed a pattern.

Khaled began to feel strangely tired again, a tiredness that did not match the work. He found himself explaining the decision repeatedly, each time with slightly more effort, each time noticing that his explanations landed less cleanly than they had in the meeting.

He started hearing things indirectly. A comment from someone in another part of the organisation. A sigh from a manager who had always been steady. A phrase like, "People are struggling," delivered in a way that suggested the speaker did not feel safe saying more.

Khaled called in one of his executives, Sana, a woman in her forties, and asked what was going on. Sana hesitated before answering. Not long, just long enough. "It feels like some people didn't say everything they were thinking," she said carefully. "They went quiet."

Khaled felt irritation spike, then soften into something else. "What didn't they say?" he asked. Sana looked down for a moment, then back up. "I think the room closed down," she said. "Not because you shut it down harshly, but because everyone could feel you needed it closed."

Khaled sat with that. He replayed the meeting in his mind. The polite concerns, the half-started comment, the scan for nods and the relief he had felt when the decision landed. He could not find a single point where he had been cruel. He had not intended to silence anyone. And still, he could feel what Sana meant.

The room had taken its cues from his capacity. His overload had become the ceiling for the system's honesty, his contraction had signalled that nuance was too expensive today and his desire for certainty had offered everyone the comfort of closure at the price of their full participation. No one had named the moment it closed. Not him, not them, not anyone. So the system carried it forward.

Later that week, Khaled sat in a smaller meeting with two managers who were struggling to implement the decision. Ayesha, a senior manager, and Kenji, a team leader. They spoke about resources and timelines, but beneath the words, he could sense resentment, exhaustion, perhaps a quiet grief.

He asked a question that surprised even him. "What did you want to say in that meeting that you didn't?" There was a long pause. The air thickened. Ayesha looked away. Kenji swallowed, then spoke. "It felt like you needed the decision," he said. "And we didn't want to add more mess."

Khaled nodded slowly. "And what's the mess?" Ayesha's voice tightened. "We're already at breaking point. We're trying to look competent and we're not. We're tired, scared and carrying things we can't keep carrying."

Khaled felt the words land in his body. A sensation like weight, and beneath it, something like shame. He wanted to respond, to reassure, to fix. He did not know how to do any of that without making the moment smaller again. He said nothing for a while.

The meeting ended without a clean plan. Khaled left with a sense of having discovered something too late, something that had been there in the room all along. In the weeks that followed, he made adjustments. He reopened parts of the decision. He created new forums for input. He tried, in small ways, to invite nuance back in, but the cost had already been paid. Not in disaster, not in scandal or not in explosive failure. In trust that had narrowed, honesty that now required extra effort and people who had learned, one more time, that saying less was safer.

This is how grace does not appear. Not because anyone refuses it deliberately, but because the conditions for it are quietly, even accidentally, removed.

--- o ---

Just Not Today

They were gathered for a birthday lunch that had been planned for weeks. The table looked beautiful. Food laid out carefully, generous and familiar. A kind of effort that signalled love through preparation. The house smelled of roasting and herbs. Someone had chosen flowers and someone had brought a cake. The family had learned to do these rituals well. They had become skilled at the choreography of togetherness. Hugs at the door, compliments about the meal, questions about work and weather and stories told in the safe register that keeps everyone within reach.

Underneath, though, there were fault lines. Old disagreements that had never been fully resolved. Different values, different choices, different lives. Things that could be joked about lightly, but not spoken about honestly without risking the mood.

The conflict began in a small moment, as family conflicts often do. A remark about Zara, the teenager's phone use. A criticism disguised as concern. A tone that carried impatience. Zara responded with a flash of defensiveness and an eye roll that was too big, too public. Rafiq, the father, snapped, not loudly, but sharply enough to cut.

Zara pushed back. A sentence that had been simmering for months escaped in one burst. Meena, the mother tried to calm it, but her voice carried an edge of its own. Dadi Farah, the grandmother, who had been quiet, added a comment that landed like a judgment.

Within minutes, the air had changed. Plates were still on the table, food was still being served but the atmosphere tightened. People leaned forward, voices rising and old patterns sliding into place. The argument took on a momentum that felt both inevitable and absurd.

Meena watched it unfold and felt her body flood with anxiety. She was a woman in her mid-forties, the kind who could host a room without making it obvious she was hosting it. She had done the planning, the shopping and the timing. She had smoothed the corners in advance, not only of the menu but of the mood. She had been looking forward to this lunch, not because she believed birthdays fixed anything, but because she believed in the small stitching work of being together.

Her stomach clenched. Her throat tightened. She looked at the faces around the table and saw how quickly each person had become trapped in their role. The critic, the defender, the disappointed one, the one who withdraws and the one who escalates.

She had lived this many times. Her husband, Rafiq, a man in his late forties, did not like feeling disrespected, particularly in front of his mother. He had a way of turning irritation into a crisp kind of authority that sounded reasonable, even when it was sharp. Their teenager, Zara, a girl of fifteen, was all elbows and expression lately, her moods arriving like weather, fast and unannounced, her eyes capable of saying more than her words ever would. And Dadi Farah, Rafiq's mother, in her seventies, sat upright and watchful, the keeper of standards, the guardian of what a family should look like, her disapproval rarely loud but always legible.

Meena could see the pattern assembling itself as if the table had magnets under it. She had told herself, over the years, that she wanted honesty in the family, that she wanted people to say what they felt. But she also knew how these conversations ended. With someone leaving, someone crying and days of silence afterwards. A lingering bitterness that made the next gathering harder.

She could feel the day slipping away. So she did what she always did when she felt the family tipping. She shut it down. "Enough," Meena said, with a firmness that had authority built into it. "We are not doing this today." The room went still.

Zara's eyes widened. Rafiq's mouth tightened. Dadi Farah looked away. "I'm serious," Meena continued. "We are here to celebrate. This is not the time. Drop it." The words were not cruel. They were clear. They were delivered with the force of someone trying to protect what matters. And they worked.

The argument stopped. People returned to their plates.

Someone made a joke about the food. Someone asked Zara about school. The system reassembled itself into politeness. The lunch continued. Outwardly, peace was restored.

But the peace had a particular quality to it. It was not spacious, it was controlled.

Conversation became careful and people chose safer topics. Zara spoke less, Rafiq's face stayed tight and Dadi Farah's comments became more benign, but also more distant. Everyone complied with Meena's request, and everyone, in their own way, paid the cost.

Meena felt relief, then an ache. She had saved the day. She had also, without meaning to, taught everyone that honesty was dangerous at the table.

Later, when they were clearing plates, Zara muttered something under her breath. Rafiq heard it and moved toward another clash. Meena's eyes flashed, and he stopped. A small moment, a small shutting down. By the end of the day, the family looked intact. Photos were taken, the cake was eaten and people hugged goodbye and said, "Lovely day."

Meena stood at the sink after everyone left and felt hollow. She told herself she had done the right thing. She had kept things from getting worse. And still she could feel what had been lost. Not the argument itself. The argument was not the point. The point was the moment when everyone had been close enough to touch something real, and instead had been instructed to step back into performance.

Over the next few weeks, the narrowing showed itself. Zara spent more time in her room. Rafiq grew more irritable, then quieter. Dadi Farah called less often. When she did, she spoke about safe things. Meena noticed that when anyone began to approach a difficult topic, they redirected quickly, as if they could all feel the invisible line.

The family still met. Still celebrated birthdays. Still cooked and ate and laughed. But something essential had tightened.

Meena sometimes remembered the moment she said "enough," and she felt both justified and sad. She wondered what would have happened if she had let the conflict unfold, if she had stayed present long enough for it to become something other than repetition. She also knew her own limits, how tired she was, how much she disliked the chaos of raised voices and how frightened she felt of the family breaking apart.

Her shutting down had not been malicious. It had been protective. And yet it had shaped the family. It had taught them that peace mattered more than truth, that comfort mattered more than relationship, that the price of togetherness was silence. The narrowing was quiet. That was the problem.

No one came back to name what had happened. No one said, later, "I shut that down because I was afraid." No one said, "I stayed silent because I didn't feel safe." No one said, "I wanted to keep talking."

So the family carried the pattern forward. It became normal.

--- o ---

Unanimous

The board meeting was held in a bright room with glass walls. It was meant to signal transparency, openness and modern governance. The irony of glass is that it can make people feel watched, and watched people tend to perform.

This board performed well.

The chair, Leila, prided herself on running a respectful forum. She was a woman in her early sixties, measured and composed, with the kind of voice that could smooth a room without sounding as if she was smoothing anything. She believed in civility. She had seen too many boards fracture through ego and conflict. Her style was calm, orderly and courteous. She invited contributions, summarised points, moved the agenda along. Members liked the tone. They told each other and her that it was refreshing. Meetings were efficient. Papers were dealt with. Decisions were made. People left feeling productive.

Today's agenda included a proposal that would change the organisation's direction significantly. It was framed as an opportunity. There were financial models and strategic arguments. The CEO presented it with confidence. The case was strong, at least on paper.

The CEO, Tariq, was a man in his late forties. He had a polished steadiness that helped in rooms like this, especially in rooms with glass walls, where everyone could see themselves reflected if they tilted their head slightly. He spoke clearly, moved through the slides with assurance and answered questions before they were asked. You could feel the months of preparation in his pacing.

As the presentation unfolded, Leila watched the room. She could see it in the faces. Not opposition, but hesitation. A slight tightening, a quality of silence that felt careful rather than thoughtful and a few members nodded in time with the logic, yet their eyes did not soften. One person's pen moved steadily, but their jaw looked set. Someone else stared at the screen without blinking, as if holding themselves still.

Leila knew this feeling. It was the atmosphere of competent restraint. When she opened for questions, the first contributions were mild. A clarification about assumptions. A request for more detail on timelines. A question about stakeholder reaction.

Leila felt relieved. The questions were reasonable and contained. The meeting was staying orderly and the proposal could move forward with minor adjustments. That seemed good.

Then one member began to speak and stopped. His name was Hiroshi, a man in his late fifties. Experienced, thoughtful and not prone to drama. Leila had learned to trust his instincts. When Hiroshi spoke, he usually went straight to what mattered, not to impress but to protect. He opened his mouth, then paused in a way that was almost imperceptible, as if he had felt a thought arrive and then felt something else arrive immediately after it.

Leila noticed him pause and felt a small anxiety rise. A sense that something harder might be coming. Something that could disrupt the tone.

Hiroshi smiled slightly, then reframed his thought. "Just a small concern," he said, "more a curiosity really." The concern that followed was gentle, almost apologetic. It did not challenge the heart of the proposal. It asked for reassurance that risk was being managed. Leila thanked him warmly, then turned to Tariq for a response who answered well. Leila summarised, nodded and moved on.

More questions followed in the same register. Mild, careful, polite. Anika asked about staff capacity but wrapped it in language that sounded technical, as if translating worry into an acceptable dialect. Moana asked about reputation in the market, but phrased it as a communications question, not as a deeper unease. Omar asked about regulatory implications, and looked relieved when Tariq's answer landed neatly.

Leila could feel the board converging toward approval. She asked, at one point, "Is there anything else we should be thinking about?" and the question was sincere. But her tone was light, her posture forward, her pacing brisk. The room read the cues. No one wanted to be the one who made things heavy. No one wanted to be the one who turned a smooth meeting into a complicated one.

The proposal passed unanimously. Leila smiled and Tariq looked relieved. The board congratulated itself on decisive governance. People moved on to the next agenda item with a sense of completion.

The dissent began that evening, not in public, not in the minutes, but in phone calls. Anika called Moana. "I didn't feel comfortable saying this in the meeting," she began, "but I'm worried." Worried about the organisation overreaching, reputational risk, staff capacity and that the proposal was being driven by a small group and the board had not done its job properly.

Moana admitted she felt similar. She had wanted to raise deeper concerns, but the room had felt closed. Not hostile, just sealed by politeness. It had felt as if the cost of honesty would be a loss of harmony, and harmony had become the board's unspoken value.

Omar texted Hiroshi a short message. Did you hold back today? Hiroshi replied after a while. Yes. I didn't want to be the only one making it hard.

Another member sent an email to Leila the next day, phrased carefully. It was from Moana. "Just reflecting," it said, "I wonder if we should have had more time on that item." Leila read the email and felt irritation, then a flicker of dread. Why didn't she say that in the meeting?

She replied politely, offering a follow-up conversation. Over the next week, more private concerns arrived. A call from Anika, careful and friendly, with a quiet intensity beneath it. A corridor conversation after a committee meeting, where someone said, "I'm sure it will be fine," and the words sounded like a wish rather than a belief. A note from Hiroshi asking if they could talk about "board process", which was his way of saying something was not right.

Leila began to feel as though she was holding two boards. The public board is aligned and unanimous. The private board, anxious and divided. Trust began to erode, quietly, not through conflict, but through dissonance. Members began to speak less freely in meetings, saving their real concerns for afterwards. Leila began to feel less confident in the unanimity of decisions. Tariq began to sense the undercurrent and became more guarded, more prepared, less open.

Politeness had become a form of avoidance. No one had intended this. They had simply protected the tone. The board meeting room remained bright, glass walls shining and everyone was still courteous. And yet the board had become less honest.

Grace does not appear where honesty has nowhere to go. Not because people are bad, but because the space cannot hold discomfort without rushing to tidy it.

Leila, months later, remembered Hiroshi's pause. She could see it with uncomfortable clarity now, the almost spoken thought, the quick smile, the softened edge, the way the room had accepted the smaller version of his concern like a gift. She wondered what he had been about to say.

She wondered what she had signalled in that moment, and what the room had learned from her pacing. It was hard to point to a single failure. There had been no explosion or dramatic conflict. Only a gradual thinning.

--- o ---

Trying to Help

They were lying in bed, the lights off, the room quiet enough to hear the house settle.

She had been restless all evening. Not frantic, just slightly off. A quiet tension that made small things feel heavier. He had noticed, but he was tired too. He had spent the day solving problems, managing demands and making decisions. His mind wanted an ending.

When she finally spoke, her voice was soft, as if she wasn't sure she had the right to take up space.

"I don't feel very steady," she said. "I keep worrying that I'm messing this up."

He turned toward her, attentive, ready. He loved her. He wanted her to feel better. He wanted to do the thing that would help.

"What's going on?" he asked.

She hesitated, then began to talk. About work pressures. About friendships that felt strained. About the way she sometimes felt like she was failing at being herself. Her words were not organised. They didn't follow a neat narrative. They came out in fragments, circles, half-sentences.

As she spoke, he listened with a growing urge to intervene. He could hear solutions. He could see steps. He could identify what she was doing wrong, and he meant that kindly. He wanted to help her out of the spiral.

When she paused to breathe, he began.

"Okay," he said, "here's what you need to do. First, stop taking that person's opinion so seriously. Second, you're overthinking the work thing. You're good at your job. Third, you need to sleep more. It's making everything feel worse."

He spoke calmly, reasonably, with care. He offered reassurance and inside advice.

And she went quiet.

Not abruptly. Not demonstratively. Just a subtle withdrawing, as if something in her decided to step back. Her breathing changed. Her words thinned.

He didn't notice immediately. He was still speaking, still solving.

"You just need perspective," he said. "You're letting it get to you."

She nodded in the darkness.

"Yeah," she said. "Maybe."

There was a pause.

He waited for her to continue, to feel better, to show relief.

Instead, she turned slightly away.

He felt a flicker of irritation.

I'm trying to help.

He reached for her hand. She let him hold it, but her hand felt passive, not meeting his grip. He told himself she was tired that she needed time.

The next day, the moment lingered.

She was kind, normal and functional. But something had shifted. He could sense it in small ways. The way she spoke was a little less. The way she moved through the morning was with a quiet self-containment. The way she didn't return to the topic.

Over the next week, he noticed that she stopped bringing her softer fears to him. Not deliberately. She simply learned, unconsciously, what happened when she did. When she felt unsteady, she spoke to friends instead. She journaled. She stayed quiet. She carried it alone.

Their relationship remained loving. They shared meals, laughed and made plans. Nothing broke, but the tender edge of being met in uncertainty began to disappear.

One evening, she finally named it.

"You know when I'm anxious," she said gently, "sometimes I don't need you to fix it. I need you to be with me in it."

He felt a flush of shame. He could feel his own defences rise, his impulse to explain himself.

"I was trying to help," he said.

"I know," she replied. "That's the problem. You go straight to helping."

He sat with that, and in sitting with it, he could feel the truth of it. His advice had been a way of managing his own discomfort. Her uncertainty had made him uneasy. He had reached for competence to calm himself.

Advice is not always unloving. Often, it is care expressed through the only language someone knows.

But in that moment, it had bypassed her need.

She had reached for reassurance, for companionship, for the quiet message that she didn't need to become more organised to be held.

He had offered a technique.

Something in her had withdrawn, not out of spite, but out of self-protection. She had learned, in her body, that this space could not hold her in that way.

The cost was not visible. It did not show up as an argument. It showed up as a narrowing of intimacy.

Later, in bed again, he tried to do it differently. When she spoke of worry, he said less. He listened longer. He held her hand and stayed.

It was awkward for him at first. He could feel how much he wanted to move toward resolution. He could feel how exposed he felt in silence.

And sometimes he still failed. Sometimes he still rushed.

But he could not escape the recognition now. That love can harden too, when it insists on fixing what needs holding.

--- o ---

You Should Know Better

It was late, and the house was quiet.

He had done what needed to be done. The day had been full, the kind of day that leaves you buzzing even after you stop moving. He should have been able to sleep, but his mind kept replaying a moment from earlier, a small interaction that wouldn't have mattered to anyone else.

He could see it clearly; there was a slight hesitation before he spoke, an awkward phrasing and the look on someone's face. The way the conversation had shifted after that was subtle but unmistakable. He felt the familiar heat of embarrassment, then the heavier feeling underneath it.

You should know better.

The thought arrived quickly, with the sharpness of long practice. It wasn't a gentle reflection, it was a verdict. He lay in the dark and felt his body tighten. The muscles in his jaw. The tension in his neck. The sinking sensation in his stomach. He began building the case against himself.

You always do this.

You're not as good as people think.

You're fooling them.

Soon they'll see it.

The mind is efficient at cruelty when it believes cruelty keeps you safe. It thinks harshness will drive improvement. It thinks judgment will prevent repetition. It thinks it is doing its job.

He did not question any of it. He accepted it as the truth. In that acceptance, something in him collapsed. Not dramatically. Quietly, a small withdrawing of vitality and a narrowing of inner space. The next breath felt shallower.

Grace requires room.

But he did not allow room. He did not offer himself curiosity. He did not ask what he was carrying. He did not consider that he was tired, overloaded, stretched thin. He reached instead for the familiar tool of self-punishment, as if punishing himself could restore control.

He could have asked, even softly, what the moment meant. He could have stayed with the feeling without turning it into a story about his worth. He could have remembered that being human includes awkwardness, includes missteps, includes learning that does not require shame.

But in that moment, none of that was available. The inner world hardened and called it discipline.

He fell asleep eventually, not soothed but exhausted. The next day, the hardness travelled with him. Not loudly, quietly.

He was slightly less generous with others, slightly more impatient and slightly more defended. He noticed faults more readily. He sought certainty where nuance would have required patience.

The self-judgement had not stayed private. It had shaped his presence. This is one of the hidden costs of grace not appearing internally. When we do not meet ourselves with space, we have less space to offer the world.

Later that week, he found himself remembering the night, and for a brief moment, he could see what had happened. Not as a failure, but as a pattern. The way overload contracted him. The way contraction reached for certainty. The way certainty became judgement. The way judgement closed the door on everything that could have softened.

It was not heroic to see this. It was ordinary. But it mattered.

Because the next time the verdict arrived, he noticed it a fraction sooner. He felt the tightening. He heard the familiar tone. He recognised the speed with which the mind moved to cruelty. Sometimes, noticing is all that becomes possible at first and that is the first crack where softness can return.

--- o ---

In none of these moments did anything explode.

That was the problem.

What hardened did so quietly, without drama or acknowledgement. By the time it was noticed, if it was noticed at all, it had already become familiar.

These are the moments that do not announce themselves as failures. They simply narrow what is possible, one closing at a time.

And because they are small, they matter more than we like to admit.

Collection III - Staying With What Is

Thirteen:

Not Knowing What to Do Next

Living without narrative closure

It was late, and the house had already settled into its night sounds. The small creaks and shifts that happen when everything else has gone quiet. He was sitting at the kitchen table with a cup of tea he had forgotten to drink, the steam long gone, the surface of the liquid dull and still.

The day had been full, but not dramatic. No crisis. No sharp conflict. Just a series of conversations that had circled something without landing. Each one had ended politely, reasonably, with a sense that more time was needed.

He had told himself that it was a good thing.

For weeks now, there had been a question sitting just out of reach. Not a technical problem. Not something that could be solved by analysis or effort. It was a question of direction, of whether to continue as things were or to acknowledge that something essential had shifted and could not be unshifted.

He had been careful not to name it too starkly. Naming it

felt dangerous, as if once spoken, it would demand a response he did not yet have the capacity to give.

During the day, he could hold it. He moved from meeting to meeting, conversation to conversation, staying present, listening, asking open questions. People appreciated that. They said it out loud. Thank you for holding the space. Thank you for not rushing us. Thank you for your patience.

Each thank you landed like evidence that he was doing the right thing.

And yet, underneath the surface calm, there was a constant low-level tension. A sensation in his body that did not ease when the day ended. A restlessness that followed him into the evening, into the quiet.

This is the first reflex at the edge.

The organism, faced with uncertainty it cannot resolve, begins to tire. It looks for relief. It longs for narrowing, for a story that will allow the nervous system to settle.

He could feel that longing now.

It would be so easy to decide. To choose a direction and justify it well. To bring coherence back to the field. He knew how to do that. He had done it many times before. He could already hear the language he would use. Measured, responsible, reassuring. He could feel the relief that would come with it, the sense of things moving again.

Alongside that relief was impatience, not toward people, but toward the ambiguity itself. Toward the way conversations kept opening instead of closing. Toward the lack of traction. Toward the feeling that time was being wasted, even though he could not quite say how.

He noticed himself becoming subtly intolerant of nuance.

When someone raised a complexity, he felt an urge to simplify it. When a conversation lingered, he felt the impulse to redirect it. When someone asked a question that opened yet another angle, he felt a flicker of irritation.

Enough now.

He told himself this was responsibility speaking. Leadership. Stewardship.

He also told himself he was staying with the question and that he was resisting the urge to force an answer too soon. That he was living with not knowing.

The story he was telling himself mattered.

That evening, alone at the table, he picked up his phone and scrolled aimlessly. Not to distract himself exactly, more to avoid the stillness that seemed to thicken the longer he sat with it. The screen lit his face briefly, then dimmed again.

He thought about the conversations he had postponed. The ones he had gently deflected with phrases like, Let's revisit this next week, or, I think we need more time with this.

Those phrases had sounded wise. Spacious. Mature.

They had also done something else.

They had closed the moment.

Not loudly. Not obviously. Just enough.

By postponing, by holding things open in theory while closing them in practice, he had relieved himself of having to feel the full weight of the uncertainty. The pressure had eased. Others had relaxed. The system had settled, temporarily.

He had mistaken that settling for staying.

The recognition did not arrive all at once. It came as a slow, uncomfortable realisation that he had already made a decision, even as he told himself he had not. The decision was not to act, but it was still a decision. One that protected him from the exposure of naming what he did not yet know how to live with.

He sat back in the chair and felt something sink in his chest.

He had missed the edge.

Not because he rushed or not because he was careless, but because he had allowed restraint to become a form of management. He had framed his hesitation as wisdom, when in truth, it was also self-protection.

The edge had been there in the moment when he felt the urge to defer, and chose instead to conclude. It had been there in the subtle relief that followed. It had been there in the way others took their cues from him and stepped back, too.

By the time he noticed, the moment had passed.

Nothing catastrophic had happened. No one was hurt. No bridges burned. And yet something essential had been lost. A chance to stay exposed together. A chance to let the uncertainty do its deeper work before being tidied away.

He could not go back to that moment now. The conversations had moved on. The field had shifted. The system had reorganised itself around the deferral.

He felt a quiet grief for that.

Not the dramatic kind. Just a low, steady sadness that comes when you realise you have traded something alive for something manageable.

There was no lesson he could extract that felt clean or comforting. No wisdom that redeemed the miss. Only the recognition that not knowing is not a stable state. It requires active presence, not passive delay. And that even then, it can slip past unnoticed.

He finished the cold tea and stood to rinse the cup. The house was very quiet now.

Tomorrow, the work would continue. Conversations would resume. Decisions would eventually be made. Life would move forward, as it always does.

But something in him had changed.

Not into certainty. Not into resolve.

Just into a deeper awareness of how easily the edge can be missed, even by those who care deeply about staying.

Especially by those who care deeply about staying.

There was no resolution here. Only the knowledge that the next time not knowing arrived, it would bring with it both possibility and risk, and that neither patience nor decisiveness would guarantee the moment would be met.

Some edges are crossed.

Others are simply passed by.

And you only realise which it was later, when the quiet has had time to speak.

Fourteen:

Fatigue That Is Not Yours

Distinguishing resonance from absorption

He noticed it first as tiredness that didn't make sense. Not the honest fatigue that follows long hours or difficult work. Not the clean exhaustion that yields to rest. This was different. It lingered. It clung. It seemed to deepen no matter how carefully he slept, how well he ate, how deliberately he slowed down. He would wake already weary, as if the night had carried on the work of the day.

At first, he treated it as a personal problem. Something to manage or something to optimise. He reviewed his habits, adjusted his routines, cut back where he could and took breaks seriously. All the sensible things. None of it touched the tiredness.

What unsettled him most was that the fatigue did not feel entirely his. It had a borrowed quality to it, as if it had arrived from elsewhere and taken up residence in his body. He could feel it settle in his shoulders during certain conversations. He noticed it spike after particular meetings. He felt it thicken when he sat with people who were themselves overwhelmed, grieving or carrying more than they could name.

He began to recognise a pattern. The tiredness intensified in moments of closeness. When people trusted him, spoke honestly and allowed themselves to lean, just a little. Fatigue, he began to suspect, was a signal. Not the whole story, but a doorway into something broader. A sign that he was taking something in that did not belong to him alone.

He had always considered himself empathic, attuned, able to read a room, sense emotional weather and notice what was unspoken. This capacity had been praised over the years, named as strength, as leadership, as care.

And it was. But somewhere along the way, attunement had slipped into absorption. The line between feeling with and feeling for had blurred. The difference between noticing emotion and becoming it had grown indistinct. He found himself carrying moods, anxieties and sorrows that were not his to resolve, yet were now living inside him as if they were.

This is how resonance works when it goes unnoticed. At its best, resonance is a form of contact, a tuning in and a way of sensing what is alive in another without losing yourself.

It is spacious, allows movement and comes and goes.

Absorption feels similar at first. That's what makes it dangerous. Absorption happens when resonance is not held consciously, empathy becomes identification, care slides into ownership and when the body quietly agrees to carry what the system, the relationship or the moment cannot. The cost of absorption is often paid in fatigue. Not because the work is too much, but because the boundary has dissolved.

He began to notice how quickly this happened, a sigh across the table, a story told with resignation rather than anger or a look that asked, without words, will you hold this for me? He felt himself respond before he had time to choose. His chest tightened, his attention narrowed and his body leaned forward, ready to take responsibility for something that had not yet been named. In those moments, fatigue was not a failure of stamina. It was the nervous system signalling overload.

There is a particular quality to suffering that is not yours. It does not arrive cleanly. It does not announce itself. It seeps in through contact, through care, through the very capacities we rely on to be human with one another. It carries the weight of grief, fear, frustration and despair that have not found a place to land elsewhere.

When suffering has no home, it looks for one. He had been offering his.

The recognition did not bring immediate relief. If anything, it sharpened his awareness of how often this exchange took place. How many times has he mistaken responsibility for compassion? How easily he assumed that feeling something deeply meant needing to do something about it.

This is where many caring people get caught. They believe that if they can feel it, they must fix it. That to notice suffering is to be accountable for its resolution. That staying present requires taking it in. None of this is true.

Presence does not require absorption. In fact, absorption often undermines presence by collapsing the very space that makes presence possible.

He began to experiment, quietly, not with techniques or defences, but with attention. When fatigue arose suddenly in a conversation, he paused inwardly and asked a simple question. Is this mine? Not as a way of distancing himself, but as a way of orienting. The question did not push the feeling away. It allowed him to place it.

Sometimes the answer was yes. Sometimes the tiredness pointed to his own limits, his own grief, his own unacknowledged strain. Those moments asked for care, rest and honesty.

But often, the answer was no. The fatigue belonged to the field. To the system. To the other person. To a shared reality that was heavy and unresolved. In those moments, something subtle shifted.

Instead of pulling the feeling inside himself, he allowed it to exist between them. He named what he noticed without owning it. He stayed with the other person without trying to relieve the discomfort prematurely. He trusted that the suffering did not need to be carried by one body alone in order to be honoured.

This was not easy. Absorption had once felt like love, competence and being needed. Letting go of it felt, at times, like withholding. Like failure. Like stepping back when something important was being offered. He had to learn that not everything offered is meant to be taken.

Distinguishing resonance from absorption is a

developmental task. It requires enough differentiation to notice what is happening inside without immediately identifying with it. Enough steadiness to allow emotion to move without capturing it. Enough humility to accept that suffering can be witnessed without being solved.

Fatigue remains the teacher here. Not the enemy, but the signal. The quiet alert that says something is being carried out of proportion. Something is being taken in rather than held.

Over time, he noticed a change. The tiredness still came, but it passed more easily. It no longer settled in his body with the same weight. He could feel emotion move through him without staying lodged there. He could care deeply without disappearing into the care. This did not make him less compassionate. It made his compassion more sustainable.

Suffering did not vanish from his world. It did not need to. The work was never about erasing pain, it was about staying present without becoming its container of last resort.

You might recognise this fatigue. The kind that doesn't lift with rest, the weariness that arrives in certain rooms or relationships or the exhaustion that feels moral rather than physical. You might pause when it appears. Not to judge yourself. Not to harden. But to ask, gently, what is being asked of you and what is simply being offered.

Some suffering needs company, naming and time. And some, quietly, needs to be returned to the world it belongs to.

Fatigue, when listened to carefully, will tell you which is which.

Fifteen:

Restraint

The courage to not act

Restraint

The courage to not act

Claire first noticed something was wrong in the way Max came through the front door.

Not slamming it. Not announcing himself. Just closing it carefully, as if sound itself might ask questions he didn't want to answer. He dropped his backpack where it always landed, by the hall table, but this time it didn't spill open. He stood there for a moment, one hand still on the strap, looking at nothing in particular.

"Hey," Claire said from the kitchen. "You're home early."

Max shrugged without meeting her eyes. "Got sent home." The words landed gently and heavily at the same time.

Claire felt the familiar surge move through her body before she had time to think. A tightening across her chest. A rush of heat. A hundred questions forming all at once, lining up, jostling for position. "What happened?" she asked, already walking toward him.

Max dropped onto the chair at the table and folded his arms, as if holding himself together. "It was stupid."

That phrase. Claire knew it too.

Stupid usually meant painful. Or humiliating. Or both.

She waited, but the waiting was thin. Fragile. Her mind was already racing ahead, assembling explanations, rehearsing phone calls, imagining meetings with teachers and counsellors and other parents whose names she barely knew but would soon.

"Max," she said gently. "What happened?"

He sighed, ran a hand through his hair and stared down at the grain of the table. "I lost it in class. Just... snapped."

Claire felt her stomach drop.

He told the story in fragments. A comment from another student that had been needling him for weeks. A teacher who didn't notice. A joke that wasn't really a joke. Laughter that wasn't friendly. Something in him was tightening, tightening, until it had nowhere left to go.

"I yelled," he said. "Said stuff I shouldn't have. Threw my

book."

Claire could picture it too clearly. The room. The eyes are turning. The heat in his face. The moment after, when the adrenaline drains and all that's left is the awareness that you can't take it back.

"They sent me to the office," he continued. "Mum, I think I'm in real trouble." There it was, the stakes. This wasn't homework. This wasn't a forgotten assignment or a late lunch order. This was reputation, belonging. The fragile scaffolding of adolescent identity that can wobble dangerously with one bad moment.

Claire felt the urge rise fast and strong. Fix it. Call the school. Explain. Contextualise. Advocate. Make sure they understood Max wasn't a bad kid. He was sensitive and he'd been under pressure. Anyone would have snapped. She had done this before, in smaller ways. She was good at it. Calm, articulate, reasonable. Adults listened to her.

She could already feel the relief that would come from acting. From doing something useful. From reclaiming control in a situation that felt suddenly precarious.

Max looked up at her, eyes flicking over her face, searching.

"What are they going to do?" he asked quietly. Claire opened her mouth. And then stopped.

She noticed something underneath the urgency. Not just fear for Max, but fear for herself. The fear of being seen as a bad parent. The fear of having failed him somehow. The fear of letting him feel pain, she could perhaps prevent.

She sat down across from him instead. "I don't know," she said. The words felt thin in her mouth.

Max frowned. "You don't know?"

"No," she said. "I don't. Yet."

He looked away again, his shoulders slumped. Claire could feel how exposed he was, how close he was to either lashing out again or folding in on himself.

This was the edge.

Version One: The rush

Claire had been here before.

In another version of this moment, she didn't pause. She moved straight into action, buoyed by competence and care. She rang the school that afternoon and asked for a meeting. Told Max to go to his room and calm down while she handled it.

She spoke carefully, explained the context, emphasised Max's usual behaviour, suggested strategies and asked about restorative conversations rather than punishment.

The school responded well. They always did. By the end of the day, there was a plan. A warning rather than a suspension. A mediated conversation. Support put in place.

Max was relieved. Grateful. "Thanks, Mum," he said, leaning into her that evening. "I don't know what I'd do without you."

Claire felt the familiar mix of pride and exhaustion.

Over the following weeks, Max stayed out of trouble. Mostly. But something subtle shifted. When things went wrong, his first instinct was to look to her, to check how worried she was and to expect she would step in.

The incident became a story about being rescued. The sharp edge of it dulled quickly. Claire noticed that when Max talked about it later, there was a hint of dismissal. "It wasn't that big a deal," he'd say. "Mum sorted it."

She felt a flicker of unease she couldn't quite name.

Version Two: The wait

This time, Claire stayed seated at the table.

Max picked at the edge of his sleeve. "Aren't you going to call them?" he asked.

Claire felt the pull again, stronger now, he needed her and he was asking. The part of her that measured love by usefulness wanted to leap in.

She didn't. "Not yet," she said softly. "I want to understand what this has been like for you."

Max's jaw tightened. For a moment, she thought he might explode. Instead, his eyes filled and he looked away quickly. "It was horrible," he muttered. "Everyone was staring. I felt stupid. And angry. And... small."

Claire felt that word land in her chest. She stayed quiet.

Max talked, haltingly at first, then more freely about the comments, the build-up, the feeling of being trapped in his own body and about how ashamed he felt afterwards. "I don't want to be that kid," he said. "The angry one."

Claire nodded. She could feel how much he wanted her to take this away. To tell him it was all okay. To promise it wouldn't stick. She resisted the urge.

"What do you think might help now?" she asked. Max shrugged, then thought. "I guess… I need to talk to the teacher, and maybe apologise, even though I'm still mad."

The words surprised both of them. Claire felt no relief this time. Her body stayed tense. She worried she was doing the wrong thing, that she was abandoning him when he needed her most.

The next day was hard. Max met with the school on his own, though Claire was invited to attend if she wanted. She waited at home instead, phone beside her, resisting the urge to rehearse what she'd say if it rang.

When Max came back, he looked older somehow. Not happier, not lighter, but steadier. "I got a suspension," he said. "Three days."

Claire inhaled slowly. She let the fear wash through her without pushing it onto him. "And?" she asked.

"They listened," he said. "It sucked, but they listened and I said my piece." He paused. "I'm embarrassed. But… I think I needed it."

Claire nodded. That evening, they sat together on the couch. Not talking much. Just being near. Max leaned against her, the way he had when he was younger, before he pretended he didn't need that anymore.

"You didn't fix it," he said quietly. Claire smiled, just a little. "No."

"I'm kind of glad," he added after a while.

She didn't reply. There was nothing to add.

The situation didn't resolve neatly. The suspension happened, the whispers faded slowly and Max still had bad days. Claire still felt the urge to intervene sometimes, especially when she saw how heavy it all felt on him.

But something had shifted, not in the world, but in Max and in her. Restraint, she was learning, was not about doing nothing. It was about not stealing an experience that belonged, painfully and importantly, to someone else. Some days that felt wise. Other days, it felt cruel. Most days, it just felt hard.

The work continued. So did the waiting, and somewhere in that waiting, without announcement or applause, something in Max began to settle into its own shape.

Sixteen:

Collapse and Return

Losing presence and finding it again

The room was full in that particular way that only an all-staff meeting can be full.

Not just chairs and bodies and coffee cups, but history. Stories. Tensions carried quietly for months. Expectations that sat like weights in people's laps. The accumulated hum of a system that had been through more than it liked to admit.

The CEO, James, stood at the front with a microphone clipped too high on his shirt and a clicker in his hand that felt strangely small for what he was about to hold. Behind him, the screen glowed with a slide that said something hopeful and tidy, a plan, a timeline and a set of bullet points that made it all look more manageable than it felt.

The first ten minutes went well. James spoke calmly. He acknowledged pressure, thanked people for the work they'd done, made a few gentle jokes about the weather and the coffee. People laughed politely, a few genuinely. The room breathed a little.

The system, in its own way, was testing him. Is he steady? Can he hold us? James had been learning to read that question not as an accusation, but as longing. People wanted to trust and wanted to protect themselves from disappointment.

He moved into the harder part. The part that always changed the air. "Today I want to speak about the next phase," he said, and he felt the room tighten just slightly. "The reality is we need to make some decisions that will affect workload and priorities. We can't keep carrying everything."

He clicked to the next slide. A murmur moved along the back row, the sound of paper shifting, someone whispering to a neighbour. James felt his shoulders tighten. He didn't like the murmur as it felt like resistance or worse, dismissal.

He knew, intellectually, that murmurs were normal. People are reacting, trying to orient. But his body didn't interpret it that way. His nervous system read it as a threat. He pressed on, a little faster than before. His voice sharpened and he started using the language of certainty. "We will do this. We must do that. The deadlines are non-negotiable."

He could feel himself leaning forward, pushing the room

rather than meeting it. The energy in his chest rose, a hot, contained urgency that wanted the meeting to behave.

Somewhere near the third slide into the "non-negotiables," someone raised a hand. James nodded curtly. "Yes."

A woman in the second row stood. Her voice was steady, but there was emotion underneath it. "James, I'm trying to understand how this is going to work in reality. We're already at capacity. You're asking for more without taking anything away."

It was a fair question. A necessary question.

James heard it as a challenge. He felt the flash before he could stop it, the reflexive surge of defensiveness disguised as authority. A line formed in his mind, sharp and dismissive. We've explained this.

He opened his mouth and it came out harsher than he intended. "We can't keep saying we're at capacity every time we need to change," he said. "At some point, we have to adapt. That's what we're here for."

The room went quiet in a way that did not feel respectful. It felt like a door closing. James saw faces shift; some looked down, some stared and someone in the back crossed their arms. The woman who had asked the question sat slowly, eyes fixed on the floor, as if she had been physically pushed back into her chair.

James felt a rush of satisfaction, then almost immediately, a wave of something else.

Shame.

Not the dramatic kind that collapses you, but the quiet, sickening recognition that you've stepped over your own values and you can't pretend you didn't.

He kept going anyway. That was the old move. If you've said something harsh, you double down. You keep the meeting moving. You don't stop and draw attention to the crack. You don't let people see you wobble.

He clicked to the next slide. His hand shook slightly as he did. That was when he noticed his breath, shallow and high in his chest. His jaw was clenched and he could feel his face flushed. He was speaking, but he couldn't quite hear himself. The words were there, but the presence had gone. He was performing leadership, not inhabiting it.

James paused mid-sentence. He could feel everyone watching him now, waiting to see what he would do next.

The system leaning in, just stopped. The silence was not comfortable. It arrived with weight, like a rock placed deliberately in the path. This was not the planned agenda.

James swallowed. He took the microphone off his shirt and held it in his hand, as if that small physical shift might help him shift internally too. "I need to pause," he said. The words sounded strange, almost too plain for a CEO in front of staff. Not strategic or polished, just true.

"I just felt myself… tighten," he continued, and he could hear his own voice soften as he spoke. "And I think I responded in a way that wasn't fair."

He looked toward the woman who had asked the question. She was still staring down. "I'm sorry," he said, clearly this time. "That came out sharp. You asked a reasonable question and I answered from defensiveness. I want to own that."

The room did not move. People barely breathed. James felt exposed, the old part of him wanted to retreat, to turn the apology into a quick line and move on.

But something in him stayed. He took a slow breath, this one went lower. "What happened in me just then," he said, "is that I heard the question as resistance. My body went into threat and I reached for authority to shut it down." He paused again, letting the words land without rushing to tidy them away. "That's not the kind of leadership I want to practise here," he continued. "It's not what you deserve. And it's not what will help us do hard things together."

He looked out across the room, not scanning for approval, but actually seeing. People's faces were a mixture of surprise and caution, as if they didn't trust what they were witnessing yet.

"I'm going to try again," he said. "And I'm going to do it more slowly."

In the third row, Amelia felt her own body tense with an impulse she had been practising against for months. Rescue. Amelia was one of James's strongest supporters. She believed in him, had seen him do difficult things with integrity and had also seen the way this organisation could turn on leaders when they showed weakness.

When James snapped at the woman in the second row, Amelia's stomach had clenched. She had felt the familiar panic, the fear that the meeting would spiral. The old organisational story would awaken. Here we go, another

CEO who talks about care, then shows the steel when challenged. Amelia's instinct had been to intervene. To soften the moment on his behalf. To crack a joke. To say something supportive. To redirect attention so James didn't have to sit in the awkwardness. She almost raised her hand. Then she saw him stop.

When he apologised, Amelia felt a rush of warmth and dread at the same time. Warmth, because something real was happening. Dread, because she knew how people could interpret it. How easily vulnerability could be weaponised. How quickly someone might decide he was unsafe or weak. Her rescue impulse rose again, stronger. Don't leave him alone up there.

She gripped her notebook instead, fingers tight around the edges. She forced herself to stay seated. To let James hold his own repair. To trust that this wasn't her moment to manage. Her whole body wanted to move. She stayed still. It felt like holding her breath underwater.

Across the room, near the back, Mark watched with narrowed eyes. Mark had been at the organisation long enough to have seen leaders come and go. Each arrival had begun with warmth, promises, a vision of partnership. Each departure had left a residue of cynicism. Mark's nervous system had learned to protect him by expecting disappointment.

When James snapped, Mark felt vindicated. There it is. He felt his shoulders drop, the kind of drop that comes with bleak confirmation. He could almost hear his own inner voice, dry and weary. True colours. We're not safe. He'll talk about collaboration until someone pushes, then the hammer comes out. Mark had already decided what the rest of the meeting would be. More polished slides. More "we're all in this together" language. More pressure dressed up as care.

Then James stopped. Mark frowned. He felt suspicion first. This is a tactic. A performance, a quick apology to regain control. He watched closely, waiting for the pivot, the strategic reframe and the way leaders say sorry without really being sorry.

But James didn't pivot. He explained what happened in his body, named defensiveness, didn't blame the room or the question. Mark felt something shift, just slightly, like a muscle unclenching. He didn't trust it yet. He watched the woman in the second row. She still hadn't looked up.

James turned toward her again, gently. "Would you be willing to ask the question again?" he said. "Or if not, I can repeat it, because it matters." The woman lifted her head slowly. Her eyes were bright and she nodded once. "I just… I don't see how we do this without breaking people," she said, voice quieter now. "I want to support the direction. I just need you to see what it's like on the ground."

James nodded. "I do need to see it," he said. "And I need you to keep telling me, not as resistance but as reality."

He looked out again. "Let's do this together," he said. "Not in the pretend way. In the actual way."

The room breathed. Not everyone, not fully but enough.

James felt something returning. Not confidence, exactly. Not certainty.

Presence.

His shoulders softened. His voice lowered. He stopped pushing the slide deck like it was a shield. He asked more questions. He allowed longer pauses. He let staff name what was hard without immediately correcting them.

The meeting became slower and less tidy. It also became more alive. People spoke from experience rather than from rehearsed positions. The cynicism in the room did not disappear, but it loosened enough for curiosity to peek through.

Mark found himself leaning forward, almost against his will. He didn't speak, not yet, but he stopped scrolling on his phone. He looked at James's face. It didn't look polished, it looked human.

Amelia felt tears prick her eyes, surprising her. Not because the moment was sentimental, but because it was rare. To watch someone in authority lose presence, name it and return without making it someone else's problem. She felt proud of him. She also felt something like relief for the whole system as if the organisation had been waiting for this kind of repair and didn't quite know it.

When the meeting ended, people didn't leap up immediately. They moved slowly, talking in low voices. There were no standing ovations, no clear victory. Just a different quality in the air, as if something had been allowed that was usually forbidden.

James stayed at the front for a while, packing up his notes with hands that were still slightly unsteady. He felt drained and strangely clear. He hadn't saved the meeting. He hadn't solved the organisational pressures. He had simply returned.

The next day, Mark mentioned the moment to a colleague in the kitchen, trying to sound casual. "Did you see him stop?" he asked. The colleague shrugged. "Yeah. Weird." Mark hesitated, then said quietly, "Maybe not weird. Maybe... different."

Amelia, later, wrote James a short note. Not praise, not reassurance, just acknowledgement. I saw the return. James read it once, then again, and put it away carefully.

The story did not end there. Repair rarely ends with one meeting. People would test him again. The system would lean again. His nervous system would tighten again. There would be other collapses, some caught, some missed.

But something had been demonstrated in public. Not perfection, return.

And perhaps that is the more important capacity. Not to stay present always, which is a fantasy, but to notice when presence is gone, to name it without theatre and to find a way back without demanding that others carry the cost.

Grace did not arrive like light streaming through clouds. It arrived as a pause, an apology and a man standing in front of a room choosing, in real time, to come back to himself.

Seventeen:

Joy Without Apology

Holding joy alongside suffering

The laughter escaped Lena before she could decide whether she meant it.

It rose up from somewhere low in her chest, brief and unguarded, and startled her as much as anyone else in the room. For a moment, she felt the unmistakable lift of it, the body remembering something it had not been using much lately. Then, almost immediately, came the recoil.

Too much. Too soon. Not here.

Lena felt herself pull back from the sound of her own laughter, as if it had betrayed her. She lowered her eyes and pressed her lips together, trying to fold herself back into the shape the room seemed to require.

The room was small, ordinary. A community hall with stacked chairs against the wall and a kettle that never quite boiled fast enough. A circle of people who had arrived carrying things they did not know where else to put. Loss, weariness and grief that had become part of the furniture of their lives. They were not here to feel better. They were here because feeling nothing at all had begun to feel worse.

Lena had come because her sister, Eva, had died six months earlier. Cancer, fast and unforgiving. The kind of death that rearranges time and makes joy feel like a foreign language. She had learned, in the months since, how quickly aliveness could feel like a transgression.

The facilitator had been speaking about memory, about the strange details that linger. She mentioned her late husband's habit of writing grocery lists that made no sense. Milk. Milk. Milk. No bread. No dinner.

That was when Lena laughed.

It wasn't the list itself. It was the way Eva used to do the same thing. The way she'd stand in the kitchen, pen in mouth, frowning at the fridge as if it were withholding information. The way she'd laugh at herself when she forgot something obvious. The laughter carried all of that with it.

For Ruth, sitting across the circle, the sound landed hard. She felt it register in her body as a sharp tightening, a quick defensive bracing she knew well. Her husband had been dead for three years. She had learned to keep grief close and joy at a distance. Joy felt reckless, disloyal, like stepping out of line when everyone else was standing still.

When Lena laughed, Ruth's first thought was sharp and unforgiving. How can she? The thought embarrassed her even as it arrived. Ruth prided herself on being generous, compassionate, but grief had narrowed her. It had taught her to protect the pain as if it were sacred. Joy, when it appeared, felt like a threat.

Lena felt the room go quiet and interpreted it instantly as judgement. Her chest tightened, her breath became shallow and she wanted to apologise, to explain herself back into acceptability.

"I'm sorry," she began, the words already half-formed. The facilitator held up a hand, not abruptly, just enough. "You don't need to apologise." Lena hesitated. She did not trust that yet.

The silence stretched, not uncomfortable exactly, but charged. Something was present that had not been invited and no one quite knew what to do with it. The facilitator spoke again, slowly. "Something important just happened," she said. "And I'd like us to stay with it, if we can." She turned to Lena. "Would you be willing to tell us what that laughter touched?"

Lena swallowed. The room felt suddenly too bright. She could feel everyone waiting, and she could also feel a pull to retreat, to give a smaller answer and keep it safe.

She didn't.

"It reminded me of my sister," she said quietly. "Not just that she's gone. But... how alive she was. How much she enjoyed being herself, even in stupid little ways." Her voice shook. "For a second, she was here. Not dying. Just... here."

The words hung in the air. Ruth felt something loosen in her chest. Not relief, recognition. She realised she had been assuming the laughter meant forgetting, moving on and leaving grief behind. What Lena was describing was the opposite. It was contact - memory with breath in it. Ruth felt tears rise, sudden and unwelcome. "I've been so careful not to feel that," she said, surprising herself by speaking. "Every time I get close to something like that, I shut it down. I tell myself it's safer not to go there."

"Safer how?" the facilitator asked gently.

Ruth shook her head. "I don't know. Like... if I let myself feel how alive he was, how much we laughed, it will break me all over again."

Lena looked at her, eyes wet. "I thought that too," she said. "But when I laughed just now, it didn't break me. It reminded me that I loved her and that I still do."

The room shifted, almost imperceptibly. Joy did not rush in. There was no lightness yet, but something opened. A small space where aliveness could sit without being chased away.

Ruth felt her body soften, just a fraction. She noticed how long it had been since she'd allowed herself to remember her husband in motion. The way he danced badly in the kitchen and the way his joy had been physical, unapologetic. She closed her eyes and felt it for a moment, not as escape, as truth.

Lena felt the shame she'd been carrying begin to dissolve. She realised how often she'd been editing herself, cutting back moments of brightness so they wouldn't offend the gravity of loss. She felt a deep, steady ache that was not only sadness. It was love, still alive.

After the meeting, they stood together by the window, watching the late afternoon light slide across the car park.

"That laugh," Ruth said quietly. "It wasn't just funny." "No,"

Lena said. "It wasn't." They didn't name what it was. They didn't need to.

Joy, when it comes honestly, doesn't ask to be defended. It doesn't erase suffering or compete with it. It stands beside it, steady and unashamed, reminding us that what has been lost once lived fully, and that we do too.

Sometimes joy arrives disguised as laughter.

If we let it deepen, it can carry us back into life without asking us to leave grief behind.

Eighteen:

Holding Competing Emotions

Sitting with the contradiction

Nina sat in her car longer than necessary, watching the café door open and close with a steady, indifferent rhythm. People came out holding takeaway cups, laughing, checking their phones, stepping back into their days without any apparent awareness that a small emotional reckoning was unfolding two metres away in a parked hatchback.

She rested her forehead briefly on the steering wheel, then lifted it again, as if checking whether that tiny gesture had changed anything. It hadn't.

Inside the café was Tom. Tom, with his crooked smile and his talent for making the worst weeks sound survivable if narrated well enough. Tom, who had once driven across town at midnight to help her move a couch that turned out to be much lighter than either of them had feared. Tom, who knew her stories so well he sometimes finished them for her, often incorrectly, and always with confidence.

Tom, who lately had been exhausting her.

The thought arrived with a jolt, followed immediately by a wave of guilt so reflexive it felt almost professional. Nina was good at guilt. She had years of practice. The idea that she might be tired of someone she loved felt like a moral failing rather than a human response.

And yet… She felt it in her body before she allowed it into words. The faint heaviness that settled in her chest when she saw his name on her phone. The small calculation that preceded answering his calls. The way she found herself half listening sometimes, nodding along while mentally scanning for an exit. At the same time, she still cared, deeply and protectively. She wanted Tom to be okay, to feel supported, known and valued. The affection hadn't diminished, if anything, that was what made the frustration sharper.

Love and irritation. Loyalty and resentment. Tenderness and the desire to run screaming into the bush with no phone reception. All of it lived there together, uninvited but stubborn.

She checked the time, sighed and got out of the car. Tom spotted her immediately and waved with the enthusiasm of someone who genuinely liked seeing her. That alone almost sent her back outside. She hugged him when he stood to greet her, noticing how familiar the shape of him still felt, how easily her body remembered this closeness even as something in her braced.

"You look serious," he said as they sat. "Should I be worried?" She smiled despite herself. "You should always be worried."

He laughed, relieved. Humour had long been their shared language, the shorthand they used to soften edges and skip over awkwardness. It had served them well. It had also, she suspected, helped them avoid certain conversations for far too long.

They ordered coffee. Tom launched into a story about work, complete with impressions of colleagues that made Nina snort before she could stop herself. For a moment, everything felt easy again. She felt the warmth of familiarity settle around them like a well-worn jacket.

Then he mentioned the call from the night before. "I think I really lost it," he said, stirring his coffee. "Thanks for staying on the phone with me. I don't know what I'd do without you." The words landed heavily.

Nina felt the familiar swell of affection and the equally familiar tightening that followed it. The part of her that wanted to be needed stood up quickly, ready to take credit. The part of her that had lain awake afterwards, staring at the ceiling with a low-grade headache and an even lower-grade resentment, made itself known too.

She took a breath, aware that this was the moment she'd been circling since she parked the car. "I care about you," she said slowly. "And I need to talk about something that's been building for me."

Tom's expression shifted almost imperceptibly. Not alarmed, exactly, but alert. As if a sensor had gone off. "Okay," he said. "That sounds... ominous."

She smiled again, softer this time. "I promise it's not a breakup. Which feels important to clarify." He laughed, a little too loudly. "Good. Because I was about to say, you don't get custody of the good mugs." That made her laugh properly, and for a moment, the tension eased.

Then she let it come back. "I've been feeling stretched," she said. "Not all the time. But enough that I can't ignore it anymore. Sometimes when we talk, I notice myself getting tired or irritated, and then I feel bad for feeling that way."

Tom frowned. "I didn't know you were irritated." "I know," she said. "I've been hiding it. I think because I didn't want to hurt you." The silence that followed was not dramatic. It was thick and sat between them like an object neither quite knew how to move around.

Tom leaned back in his chair, arms crossed loosely. Nina recognised the posture. Defensive, but trying not to look it. "So what are you saying?" he asked. "That I talk too much? That I'm a burden?"

There it was. The old pattern, surfacing quickly. Nina felt the pull to reassure, to rush in and smooth it over. To say no, no, no, of course not and make it all feel safe again. She didn't. "I'm saying I've been saying yes when I've meant maybe," she replied. "And sometimes maybe when I've meant no. That's on me, but it's catching up."

Tom stared at the table, jaw working. Nina could see the emotions moving through him even as he tried to keep them in check, hurt, embarrassment and something like fear. "Wow," he said eventually. "That's... not great to hear."

"I know," she said. "It's not great to say either." He let out a short, humourless laugh. "I always thought I was the messy one in this friendship." Nina smiled gently. "Oh, you are. I just hide mine better." That earned a real laugh from him, the kind that comes from recognition rather than deflection.

The tension shifted slightly. They talked then, slowly and imperfectly. Tom admitted he'd been leaning on her more than he realised, especially since a recent breakup he hadn't quite processed. Nina admitted she had been enjoying being the steady one more than she wanted to admit, even as it drained her. There were moments when the conversation looped, when they seemed to be talking past each other. Moments when humour bubbled up again, half-relieving, half-avoiding.

At one point, Tom shook his head and said, "It's weird. I feel defensive and relieved at the same time. Like I want to argue with you and thank you." Nina nodded. "Same. I keep wanting this to be cleaner than it is."

They sat with that for a while.

Nothing was resolved neatly. No new rules were agreed upon. No future proofing was put in place. But something had shifted in the space between them. A little more honesty, a little less performance.

When they stood to leave, Tom hesitated, then said, "I'm glad you said something. Even though I hate that you did." Nina smiled. "That feels about right."

Driving home, she noticed how her body felt different. Still tired, still tender but also lighter, as if some small internal knot had loosened. She thought about how often she had tried to simplify her inner world, to choose one emotion and silence the rest so she could act decisively. How often she had mistaken clarity for correctness.

But the truth was messier. Love did not erase frustration, boundaries did not cancel affection and humour could both connect and conceal. Staying present meant allowing all of it to exist at once, without rushing to tidy it away.

Grace, she was learning, often appeared not when things were resolved, but when contradiction was allowed to remain alive. She hadn't fixed the friendship, she hadn't broken it either. She had stayed long enough for it to breathe.

Nineteen:

Grief Without Explanation

Letting sorrow be what it is

The call came in the middle of an ordinary afternoon.

Tom was halfway through answering emails, the low-level irritation of the day humming along quietly in the background, when his phone lit up with his mother's name. He hesitated for a moment, annoyed at the interruption, then answered with the distracted warmth of someone expecting logistics or small news.

Her voice told him everything before the words did. It was his younger brother, Daniel. An accident, sudden, no warning, no illness to prepare for and no long arc of decline that might soften the shock or give grief somewhere to begin. Just gone.

Tom listened, nodded, said the necessary things. He wrote down details he didn't yet understand. When the call ended, he sat very still at his desk, hands resting on the keyboard as if they belonged there.

Nothing happened.

No tears, no collapse and no dramatic moment of realisation. Just a strange, hollow quiet, as if the world had been gently unplugged. He stayed like that for a long time, until the screen dimmed and the office noise began to feel intrusive. People laughed somewhere nearby, a printer whirred and life carried on with a confidence that felt almost offensive.

Tom stood up, collected his jacket and walked out without telling anyone where he was going.

The days that followed were thick with activity. Phone calls. Flights. Decisions. Arrangements. There was comfort in the structure of it all, in the way grief could be temporarily managed through checklists and plans. Tom moved through it efficiently, praised for his steadiness, his ability to hold things together for the family. He heard the comments and felt vaguely disconnected from them.

You're so strong.

Daniel would be proud.

At least he didn't suffer.

Everything happens for a reason.

The phrases slid off him, not because they were cruel, but

because they asked something he could not yet give, meaning, perspective or closure.

At the funeral, Tom stood at the lectern and read a short eulogy he'd written the night before. It was clear and measured. He spoke about Daniel's kindness, his stubbornness, his love of long walks and terrible jokes. People nodded, some cried, but Tom did not. Afterwards, people hugged him and whispered reassurance into his ear. He smiled politely, thanked them, felt his body go numb from the effort of staying upright.

That night, back in his childhood home, he lay awake staring at the ceiling, listening to the unfamiliar sounds of the house settling. His mind kept circling the same useless questions.

Why him?

Why now?

What am I supposed to do with this?

Each question dissolved before it reached an answer.

Days later, after most people had returned to their lives, Tom found himself sitting at the kitchen table with his aunt, Margaret. She was older, quieter than most of the others and had said very little since Daniel's death. They drank tea in silence. The kind of silence that feels companionable rather than awkward.

Finally, Margaret spoke. "I hate the way people rush grief," she said, staring into her cup. Tom looked up, surprised. "They want it to go somewhere," she continued. "To teach something, to make sense and to justify itself." She shook her head gently. "Some losses don't do that. They just break something and leave you to live with the break."

Tom felt something in his chest give way, just slightly. "I keep waiting for it to mean something," he said quietly. "Like I'm missing a step."

Margaret looked at him with a softness that didn't try to fix anything. "Grief doesn't owe us meaning," she said. "It doesn't even owe us growth. Sometimes all it asks is to be carried honestly."

That night, Tom cried for the first time, not in a rush and not dramatically. The tears came slowly, almost cautiously, as if checking whether they were allowed. He cried for the brother he had lost and for the future that would never quite look the same. He cried without insight or revelation. Without a story that made it easier.

The next morning, he woke with a dull ache behind his eyes and a heaviness in his body that felt oddly grounding. The grief hadn't lifted. If anything, it felt more present, but it was no longer abstract.

Over the weeks that followed, Tom noticed how often people tried to help by explaining, reframing or looking for silver linings. He also noticed how exhausting it was to resist those invitations. Sometimes he accepted them, just to make conversations easier, sometimes he nodded and said nothing and occasionally, when he trusted the person, he told the truth.

"I don't need it to make sense," he'd say. "I just need room to miss him." Not everyone understood. Some looked uncomfortable, as if he were breaking an unspoken rule. Others softened, relieved to be released from the pressure to offer wisdom.

Tom began to understand that grief was not a problem to solve, but a condition to live alongside. It had rhythms. Some days it was sharp and intrusive, other days it receded enough for ordinary life to resume. There was no progress line or clear movement forward. And slowly, without announcement, he stopped trying to explain it.

He stopped asking what it was for and let it be what it was.

Grief without explanation is not resignation or despair. It is a form of honesty that refuses to decorate loss, so it will be easier to tolerate. It is allowing sorrow to take up the space it requires, neither rushing it nor romanticising it.

Sometimes grace appears not in the easing of grief, but in the permission to stop making sense of it, to sit with what cannot be repaired and to live on, carrying the absence, without needing it to justify itself.

178

Collection IV — Holding Lightly

There comes a time when effort stops being the answer.

Not because effort has failed, but because it has done its work. Skills have been learned, positions have been held and patterns have been repeated often enough to be recognised. What once required striving now asks for something quieter.

This part of the book sits there.

Not at the end of a journey and not at its beginning. More like a long stretch of road where the scenery changes slowly and the questions become less urgent but more enduring. The work is no longer about getting somewhere. It is about how you travel with what you are already carrying.

Somewhere along this stretch, a subtle shift often occurs. The move is not announced and it is rarely chosen outright. People begin to turn toward you differently. Less for answers, more for steadiness. Less for instruction, more for how you are with things. The posture of the expert loosens and something closer to an elder begins to emerge, not as an identity to claim, but as a way of being noticed.

Power is still present here, so is love, but they are no longer clenched. They are handled with a little more space around them. Less urgency to prove, less need to be certain and more willingness to stay with what cannot be resolved or fixed or finally secured.

With this shift comes expectations. Sometimes spoken, often not. The expectation that you will know, carry, be calm, generous, available and hold what others cannot, simply because you can. Learning to live with those expectations, without being captured by them or withdrawing from them, becomes part of the work.

Holding lightly is not indifference, it is not withdrawal and it is not the loss of care. It is what becomes possible when you no longer need power to reassure you or love to redeem you, when ego is recognised as a companion rather than an enemy. When limits are no longer read as failure. When grace is understood not as something to be cultivated, but as something that arrives when it is allowed to.

The chapters that follow do not offer conclusions. They reflect conditions many people recognise but rarely name. The moment when competence no longer satisfies, the quiet loosening of ambition and the strange relief that comes with no longer being the centre of the story.

Nothing here is urgent. Nothing is promised. This is simply an invitation to notice how things are held now and what changes when they are held a little more lightly.

Twenty:

When Competence Is No Longer Enough

The quiet shift from skill to capacity

For most of his working life, David had been good at things, not in a flashy way and not the kind of brilliance that dazzles and exhausts in equal measure. His competence was steadier than that, dependable and trustworthy. The sort of competence that makes people exhale when you enter a room.

David was the one who read the brief properly. Who asked the clarifying question before the problem metastasized? Who noticed when timelines didn't quite line up and fixed them quietly before anyone else needed to know there had ever been an issue. He didn't seek attention for it. He simply took satisfaction in the feeling that things made sense when he was involved.

Competence had been his language in the world. It shaped his identity in ways so gradual and rewarded that he barely noticed it happening. Each success reinforced a particular posture toward life: pay attention, work it out, take responsibility, be useful. Over time, usefulness became not just something he did, but something he *was*.

When people came to him with problems, he felt a familiar internal settling. This was his place, where he belonged and he knew how to be here. Competence gave him more than professional standing. It gave him orientation. It answered questions he didn't know he was asking.

Who am I in this room? The one who understands.

Why do I matter here? Because I can help.

What is expected of me? That I will know or quickly learn, what to do next.

The world rewarded this identity generously. Promotions arrived, trust accumulated and his name was mentioned in rooms he wasn't yet in. He became someone others leaned on, sometimes without realising they were doing so.

And David leaned into it. He learned to equate steadiness with worth, clarity with care and preparation with safety. When things were messy, his instinct was to bring order. When people were anxious, he translated complexity into steps and plans.

It worked. Until, slowly, it didn't. The shift did not announce itself with failure or humiliation. There was no dramatic fall from competence, no public mistake that forced reflection. His performance remained strong, reputation intact. From the outside, the arc looked uninterrupted.

From the inside, something began to thin. David noticed it first in his body. A low level tension that didn't resolve when tasks were completed, tightness in his chest during conversations that used to energise him and restlessness that surfaced when problems refused to yield to logic or effort. He found himself growing impatient in meetings that circled without conclusion. He felt a subtle irritation toward people who spoke from uncertainty or emotion rather than analysis. He caught himself thinking, not unkindly but definitively, We're not getting anywhere. What he didn't yet recognise was that the work itself had changed.

The problems now arriving in his field were not technical, they were human, involving competing values, unspoken histories, identity and fear. They did not submit to expertise in the way earlier challenges had. No amount of preparation could fully anticipate them and no framework could hold them neatly. David responded as he always had: by sharpening his competence. He read more, attended additional training, refined his language, stayed later, prepared more thoroughly and spoke with greater authority. If clarity wasn't emerging, he assumed he simply hadn't thought hard enough yet.

For a while, this helped. Or at least it postponed the reckoning. Then came the weariness. Not burnout exactly. More of a quiet dissatisfaction, he didn't know how to name. A sense that he was working harder for diminishing returns. That his answers were landing, but not transforming. That people were listening, but not shifting.

He began to notice a subtle loneliness in his role. People brought him their problems, but rarely their uncertainty. They expected him to hold things together, not to sit with them while they fell apart.

Competence, he realised, had begun to isolate him. It had shaped an identity that was strong, capable and increasingly alone.

The moment that finally named the shift came in a conversation that felt ordinary at first. He was meeting with Maya, a colleague he respected deeply as thoughtful and grounded. Someone who didn't rush to certainty. They were discussing a project that had stalled under the weight of disagreement and unspoken concern. David laid out his analysis carefully, mapped the system, named the constraints and outlined the options. His thinking was sound, he could feel it. This was good work.

Maya listened attentively, nodding as he spoke. When he finished, she was quiet. Not the polite quiet of someone waiting their turn, but the kind that signals something else is happening.

"I don't disagree with your thinking," she said finally. "But I don't feel met by it."

The words landed gently, without accusation. David felt the familiar flicker of defensiveness rise. The part of him that wanted to explain further, to clarify, to make the logic undeniable. He had the urge to demonstrate, once again, that his competence was justified.

Instead, he noticed how tired that urge felt. "What do you need?" he asked, surprising himself with the question. Maya didn't answer immediately. She seemed to be checking whether she could trust the space. "I need you to stay with the uncertainty with me," she said. "Don't solve it, just stay."

The request unsettled him more than outright criticism

would have. Staying without solving felt like dereliction, like stepping out of role. His identity tightened reflexively. If I'm not helping, what am I doing here? They sat quietly for a moment.

David became aware of his body in a way he usually avoided. The forward tilt of his posture, the held breath and the tension in his jaw that came from being perpetually ready. He let his shoulders drop slightly, not as a technique, but as an act of permission.

"I don't know what the right move is," he said. The words felt exposed, almost indecent, given how much he was known for knowing. Maya nodded. "Neither do I."

What followed was not efficient. The conversation slowed, they spoke in partial sentences, named fears without packaging them into solutions and allowed things to remain unresolved.

Nothing was decided and yet something shifted.

Afterwards, David noticed a different quality in himself. Not the satisfaction of having done well, but a groundedness that felt unfamiliar and oddly relieving. As if he had been holding his breath for years without realising it. He began to see how deeply competence had organised his sense of self. How taught him to equate value with effectiveness and subtly discouraged him from dwelling in uncertainty, from showing confusion, from admitting limits.

This wasn't arrogance, it was adaptation. A way of surviving and contributing in systems that prized clarity, speed and control.

But now, something else was being asked of him. Capacity, he began to understand, was not the same as skill. Skill was about doing. The capacity was about holding. Holding uncertainty without rushing to close it down, holding tension without transmitting it and holding other people's fear, anger or confusion without needing to fix it so he could feel competent again.

Capacity asked for presence rather than performance.

This was quieter work, less visible and harder to measure. It didn't offer the same immediate rewards.

It also carried a different kind of risk. When David stopped leading with answers, some people grew uneasy. A few wondered aloud whether he was losing his edge. Others leaned in, sensing a different kind of steadiness, even if they couldn't yet articulate it.

David himself felt unmoored at times. Without the familiar reassurance of competence, he had to relate to his own limits more honestly. He had to sit with moments where he wasn't sure what he was offering, only that he was still there.

Over time, he noticed subtle changes around him. Conversations lengthened, people spoke more tentatively at first, then more truthfully and questions surfaced that had previously been smoothed over by efficiency. The work did not become easier, it became more human.

Competence had carried David far. It had shaped him, protected him and given him a place in the world. Now it was asking to be held lightly, not discarded, not diminished, just no longer in charge.

This was the quiet shift, not from success to failure, but from certainty to presence, from being the one who knows to being the one who can stay.

Grace did not arrive as a reward for this shift. It arrived occasionally, unexpectedly, in moments when the space he was willing to hold allowed something else to emerge and when it didn't arrive, the work still felt worth doing. That, too, marked the difference between competence and capacity.

Twenty-One:

Ego as Companion, Not Enemy

Living with the inner judge without obeying it

Mark had learned the voice early, long before he knew what to call it.

It arrived as tone more than words. A slight tightening in the chest when he spoke too freely, a warm flush of embarrassment when he was noticed or a quiet recoil when he sensed someone might not approve. Over time, it gathered language and became more articulate, but the feeling of it stayed the same. It wasn't the roar of an enemy, it was the steady presence of a vigilant companion, always scanning the edges for danger, always trying to keep him inside the lines of belonging.

What Mark did not see, for a long time, was that there were two presences growing up inside him, not just one.

One was the judge, the part that watched and evaluated, measured and warned, kept score and kept him small. The other was his ego, not as vanity, not as arrogance, but as the part of him that organised his identity. The part that decided who he was allowed to be in the world. The part that tried to make a coherent life out of all the signals he received about what earned love and what risked loss.

The ego had begun as a good, practical thing. A young boy's attempt to find footing. A way to stay connected to the people who mattered. A way to belong without bleeding.

It learned quickly. It noticed what drew warmth and what drew correction. It noticed when adults softened and when they tightened. It noticed which versions of Mark were welcomed and which were subtly managed. Over time, it built a self that was not false, just edited. A self with sharp edges filed down. A self that could survive.

As he grew older, the voice seemed to split into two parts. One part was practical. It helped him read rooms, reminded him to prepare and nudged him to consider other people's perspectives before he charged ahead. It was the part of him that had learned, with care and intelligence, how to move in the world. The other part was harsher, sharper and oddly intimate. It didn't just advise, it judged. It didn't merely warn him of risk, it threatened him with humiliation.

It knew him too well. It knew exactly where to press:

Don't say that.

That will sound needy.

That was too much.

You should know this by now.

Who do you think you are?

What made it so difficult to resist was that the inner judge rarely made things up entirely. It drew on real data. It quoted back his own mistakes. It pointed out patterns he could not honestly deny. It reminded him of moments he wished he could erase and the subtle ways he sometimes did push too hard, talk too long and hide when he wanted to be brave.

There was always a grain of truth in what it said. And that was the trap.

Mark learned to accept not just the information, but the attack that came with it, as if the cruelty was part of the accuracy. As if the only way to stay safe and improve was to let himself be spoken to with contempt.

Here is where ego quietly entered the story and tightened its grip.

Because the judge was not only evaluating Mark's behaviour. It was evaluating his right to exist comfortably in the room. It was questioning his worthiness of belonging. And Mark's ego, the part responsible for keeping him intact, took that personally. It did what egos do when threatened. It tried to manage the threat.

Sometimes it managed it by becoming competent. Sometimes by becoming helpful. Sometimes by becoming impressive. Sometimes by becoming invisible. Always, in one way or another, by trying to secure acceptance.

In his younger years, this had helped him or it had seemed to. He became competent, careful and thoughtful. He learned how to anticipate expectations, how to be useful and how to stay just inside the boundaries of what was acceptable. Praise came often enough to reinforce the strategy. People described him as steady, insightful and grounded. They trusted him and sought him out.

The role suited him. It gave him a place to stand. It also trained him to edit himself. Not in an obvious, calculating way, but in the small habitual ways that happen when you learn that being fully seen carries risk. He learned to soften his opinions before they could offend, compress his feelings into something palatable and keep his longing and uncertainty out of view. The inner judge hovered in the background like a strict tutor, correcting his posture, adjusting his tone and telling him when he had revealed too much.

And his ego, trying to keep him safe and coherent, began to bind itself to that edited self.

Competence was not just something he did. It became a way of being. It became the language through which he earned a place. It became the evidence he offered, silently and constantly, that he deserved to be included. It shaped his identity so gradually he barely noticed it happening, until one day he could not tell where the skill ended and the self-began.

As Mark grew into leadership, the judge simply updated its standards. It became less concerned with whether he would be liked and more concerned with whether he would be respected. It told him not to be weak, arrogant, hesitant, needy and certainly not to fail.

His ego nodded along, not because it agreed with the cruelty, but because it recognised the stakes. If respect was the currency now, then respect had to be protected. If failure risked exposure, then failure had to be prevented. If uncertainty looked like weakness, then uncertainty had to be managed.

It was exhausting, but it also felt familiar. Mark assumed this was just what adulthood required. He imagined everyone lived with some version of this low-level commentary, the internal supervision that kept you functioning. He also assumed, quietly, that one day it might ease. That if he became good enough, careful enough and impressive enough, the voice might soften.

It didn't.

The moment that changed his relationship with it arrived without drama, as these moments often do. It arrived one evening when he was sitting alone after a long day, not doing anything in particular, simply letting the day drain out of him.

There was no crisis, no argument or no decision. Just a quietness in which the voice, no longer kept at bay by activity, stepped forward:

> You could have handled that meeting better.
>
> Why did you say it that way?
>
> They probably think you're incompetent.
>
> You're going to be found out eventually.

Mark felt the familiar tightening begin. The urge to replay the meeting, correct himself internally and promise that next time he would get it right.

And then, unexpectedly, he felt something else. Weariness, yes, but also a kind of gentle curiosity. The thought was simple and almost tender.

What are you trying to do for me?

He sat with that question without demanding an answer. He didn't argue with the voice, just stayed long enough to feel what lay underneath it. The answer came as sensation rather than words, like a low humming vigilance that never quite turned off.

The judge wasn't trying to destroy him. It was trying to protect him, and then another layer became visible, as if the room inside him had widened.

His ego was not only listening to the judge. It was organising his whole identity around the judge's warnings. The ego had built a self that could survive the imagined consequences. It had done this with intelligence, with discipline, with a kind of devotion. It had carried him across years.

He could feel that devotion now. He could feel the

earnestness of it. The ego did not want praise for its work. It wanted safety. It wanted steadiness. It wanted a life in which he could belong.

The realisation didn't make the voice disappear, didn't turn it into a friendly guide overnight, but it shifted its temperature. Mark began to see the inner judge not as a monster in the basement, but as an overworked security guard who had been on duty far too long. It had learned, early, that exposure could bring pain, being fully oneself could lead to rejection and the safest approach was to stay small enough, polished enough and careful enough to be accepted.

It had kept him safe. It had also kept him small.

And his ego, the part of him tasked with keeping his life coherent, had taken the judge's standards and turned them into identity. It had made a deal that was never spoken aloud.

If I perform competence, I will be safe.

If I manage perception, I will belong.

If I stay impressive enough, no one will see the tender parts that might be rejected.

Mark began to notice how often he obeyed the voice without question. How reflexively he adjusted his behaviour to appease it. How quickly he withdrew when he sensed disapproval. How often he measured his worth against an invisible audience whose standards were never stable.

The judge offered him a cruel bargain: if you listen to me, you will avoid shame.

But Mark had been listening for years and shame still found him. Not because he was doing everything wrong, but because the inner judge needed shame to justify its authority. And the ego, loyal and pragmatic, kept feeding the judge evidence that its job was necessary.

The next shift came slowly, through small experiments rather than grand decisions. The first experiment was simply noticing the difference between information and attack. The voice would say, you talked too much in that meeting and Mark could feel the truth in it. Yes, he had. He had filled space because he felt anxious and had over-explained because he wanted to be understood.

But then the voice would add, You're an idiot and that part was not information. It was violence.

Mark began to practise separating them. He would take the first part in, the grain of truth that could actually help him. Then he would set a boundary around the second part, the attack that wanted to crush him into compliance. Sometimes he did this internally with surprising simplicity.

Yes, I spoke too long. That's useful to know.

No, I'm not going to talk to myself like that.

This was where the ego began to change its role.

In the old pattern, the ego had treated the judge as the authority and treated shame as the price of improvement. Now the ego began to act like a steward instead. It began to hold a boundary. It began to learn a new kind of strength, not the strength of performance, but the strength of self-respect.

It felt strange at first, almost indulgent. As if refusing the attack meant refusing responsibility. But he began to notice the opposite was true. When he accepted the grain of truth without the attack, he was more able to learn, more able to apologise and more able to adjust. He didn't have to defend himself against himself or collapse in order to improve.

The second experiment was letting himself be seen a little

more, even when the judge tightened.

The voice would say, Don't share that, it will sound needy. Mark would feel the tightening in his chest, the urge to retreat. Sometimes he would retreat, he was not trying to be heroic. But sometimes, when the moment mattered, he would speak anyway.

Not dramatically, not defiantly, just honestly.

The world did not collapse. Some people leaned in, some didn't.

A few looked uncomfortable and a few looked relieved, as if they had been waiting for him to stop performing competence. The voice responded quickly, as it always did. See? Too much. And Mark, for the first time, didn't rush to believe it. Maybe for them, he thought and felt how quietly radical that was. Not because he wanted to dismiss others, but because he was beginning to understand that being acceptable to everyone was not the same as being at home in himself.

This was ego work too, though he would not have called it that. Because ego, in its healthier form, is not the part that demands admiration. It is the part that can hold a stable sense of self in the face of mixed feedback. It is the part that can tolerate being misread without collapsing, can tolerate disappointing someone without making it mean he is unsafe.

Mark also began to see how impossible the judge's standards were. There would always be people for whom he was too intense, too reflective, too slow or too direct. There would always be people for whom he was not bold enough, not decisive enough and not impressive enough.

The judge promised safety if he could just find the right setting. There was no right setting.

And his ego began, slowly, to stop bargaining with the world. It began to stop auditioning.

What changed was not the voice, but Mark's relationship to it. He stopped trying to eliminate it. He stopped treating it as an enemy to be conquered. He began to treat it as a companion who had done its job for a long time and now needed firmer boundaries. He started responding to it with a kind of steady kindness.

Thank you, he would think, when it tightened. I see what you're worried about and I'm not going to let you speak to me like that.

Sometimes the judge quietened. Sometimes it kept going, doubling down. Mark learned he didn't need it to agree with him in order to stop obeying it. He could carry its worry without handing it the steering wheel, and he began to understand something that softened him further.

The judge was not only cruel. It was also informed. It was, in a warped way, skilled.

It knew where the truth was. It knew the moments he had overreached, the times he had avoided, the patterns he tended to repeat when anxious. It offered him useful information, often with surgical accuracy.

The problem was the delivery. The judge would bring a grain of truth in one hand and a weapon in the other.

Mark began to practise receiving one and refusing the other.

Yes, there is something to learn there.

No, you don't get to attack me while I learn it.

At first, it was clumsy. Sometimes he swallowed the weapon along with the truth without noticing. Sometimes he rejected everything and called it all self-criticism, even the part that could have helped him grow. The old habits were strong.

But over time, he became more discerning.

He began to sense, in his body, when the judge was offering information and when it was trying to punish. The first felt clean, even if uncomfortable. The second felt hot, humiliating and contracting. When he could tell the difference, he could do something new.

He could accept the truth and set a boundary around the contempt. That boundary became a kind of quiet dignity. A stable place inside him that did not need to win arguments with the judge, did not need to banish it, just needed to stop consenting to its cruelty.

There were still moments of self-doubt, days when old patterns reasserted themselves and times when he walked away from an interaction replaying it in his head, wincing at what he'd said or what he hadn't. But something fundamental had shifted.

Mark no longer took the inner judge as truth. He saw it as information mixed with fear. He learned to accept the information and refuse the cruelty. He noticed how much lighter his body felt when he didn't collapse around self-judgement. How much more present he was when he stopped monitoring himself from the outside. He noticed that people responded differently when he was less edited. Some drifted away, uncomfortable with the change, others came closer and a few relationships became more honest, more spacious.

He felt less driven to be liked and more interested in being real.

This wasn't confidence in the performative sense. It wasn't the loud assurance of someone who believed they were exceptional. It was quieter than that. It was the contentment of someone who knew he would be too much for some people and not enough for others and could live with that without flinching. It was the relief of no longer needing to audition for belonging.

Grace did not arrive when Mark finally perfected himself or silenced the voice.

Grace arrived when he stopped fighting his own humanity, when ego became a companion rather than an enemy. When the ego stopped mistaking the judge for the ruler of his worth and began to hold a steadier centre. When the inner judge was acknowledged, listened to for the truths it carried and then gently refused when it tried to turn those truths into weapons.

In that refusal, something settled. Not superiority, not certainty. A steadier relationship with himself. And from that steadiness, a freedom to meet the world with less armour, less apology and less need to be anything other than who he already was.

Twenty-Two:

Ageing, Limits and the End of Proving

When achievement stops organising meaning

On the morning Paul turned sixty-four, he woke before the alarm and lay still for a while, listening to the house. Not the dramatic listening of a man searching for revelation, just the ordinary attentiveness that sometimes comes with age, when you notice sounds you once moved straight past. A pipe clicked as it cooled, a bird called from somewhere in the dark and his partner, Elise, breathed steadily beside him, one hand tucked under her cheek in a way that still felt oddly tender after all these years.

Paul didn't feel old. He felt... familiar.

That was the strange part. The body in the bed was the same body he'd inhabited for decades, but it held itself differently now. It took longer to warm up in the mornings and he protested if he sat too long at a desk and was reminded him, sometimes with a sharp twinge in the knee or a stiffness in the lower back, that time was not an idea. It was a physical reality.

Elise stirred. "Happy birthday," she murmured, eyes still

closed. Paul smiled. "Thanks." "You're officially a distinguished elder now," she added, with the faintest edge of mischief. Paul snorted softly. "Distinguished. That's generous."

"It means you're allowed to give unsolicited advice and blame your hearing for not listening to anyone's feedback," Elise said.

Paul laughed and for a moment the day felt light. Then, as often happens, the mind did what minds do, it began to take stock. Sixty-four. It sounded like a number that should come with a verdict. A summary. A sense of what had been done and what had not. Paul found himself running through the familiar mental list, the internal ledger he'd been carrying quietly for most of his adult life.

What have you built? What have you achieved? What will remain?

He had plenty to point to. A solid career, roles that had mattered, people he had mentored and a reputation that was, by most measures, good. He had been someone, he had made things happen. And yet, lying in the half light, he felt a small, unexpected emptiness beneath all that.

Not despair and not regret, more like a loosening. There was a strange sensation that the old scoreboard wasn't as compelling as it used to be.

Paul had spent much of his life being a man with momentum. He liked targets, milestones and the clean satisfaction of progress. Achievement, for him, had not been vanity, it had been structure. It had organised his days and, in subtle ways, it had organised his sense of self.

When he was younger, proving had been obvious. Proving he could do the job, proving he belonged, proving he could lead and proving he wasn't an imposter. Proving, perhaps most quietly, that he was worthy of love and respect.

Over time, the proving became less conscious, but it didn't disappear. It just became the background rhythm of his life, like a song you don't notice until it stops. The stop began in small ways.

A few years earlier, Paul had started noticing that certain invitations no longer thrilled him. Panels, boards and roles that would have once made his pulse quicken. He found himself hesitating, not because he couldn't do them, but because he didn't want to. He hadn't known what to do with that. The old narrative told him that hesitation meant laziness, decline and loss of edge. He tried to correct it by pushing himself. Signing up, saying yes and keeping the machine of contribution running.

But his body began to object. Not dramatically, not in the form of illness that forced him to stop. It was subtler than that, which made it harder to honour. Growing fatigue after travel, longer recovery after late nights and a sense of being less elastic, less able to bounce back.

It wasn't just physical, it was emotional.

Paul began to feel a quiet intolerance for performative conversations. Meetings where everyone pretended and networking events where people spoke in polished phrases. It was as if life were a series of strategic moves. He used to play that game well enough, but now it bored him. Worse than bored him, it made him slightly sad.

He started choosing quieter things instead. Walking early in the morning, sitting with Elise in the backyard as the light shifted through the leaves and calling an old friend without an agenda. These weren't achievements. They didn't add to his identity in any visible way, yet they felt like nourishment.

Paul didn't tell many people about this shift. It was hard to explain without sounding ungrateful or self-indulgent. In a culture that prized constant contribution, he feared being seen as someone who had lost drive. So he kept proving, outwardly.

Inwardly, something kept loosening. The moment it became unavoidable came one afternoon at work. Paul was sitting in a meeting listening to a younger colleague present an ambitious plan. It was good work, energetic, sharp and future-focused. People around the table nodded enthusiastically.

Paul nodded too, at first. Then he noticed something in himself. A quiet distance, not cynicism and not superiority, just the awareness that the plan wasn't his anymore. He realised, with a strange mix of relief and sorrow, that he did not need to be the one at the centre of this, he didn't need to be the one driving. He could offer perspective, yes, support, encouragement and guidance. But the hunger to be the main force, the one who made it happen, had diminished.

He found himself thinking, almost with surprise, I'm not sure I want to win anymore. The thought startled him. Winning had been so deeply normal that he hadn't realised it was a choice.

After the meeting, Paul walked back to his office slowly. He sat down, stared at the wall for a while and felt something come up that he couldn't immediately name. It wasn't burnout or even sadness exactly. It was a kind of grief for a self he had been for a long time, an identity organised around upward movement. He didn't want to lose that self, he respected him as he had served Paul well. But he also didn't want to pretend.

That evening, Elise asked him how his day was. Paul hesitated, then said, "I think I'm changing."

Elise looked up from the chopping board. "In what way?" "I don't know," he said. "I'm just… less interested in proving and I don't know who I am without it."

Elise nodded slowly, as if the sentence made perfect sense. "That sounds like you're becoming more yourself," she said.

Paul laughed softly. "That's a very Elise thing to say."

"I'm serious," she replied. "You've spent decades being very good at being impressive. Maybe now you're allowed to be real."

Paul felt a tightening in his throat. He didn't speak for a

moment.

This was the edge.

Not a crisis, but a threshold. The end of proving does not arrive as a triumphant decision. It often arrives as a quiet question that keeps returning.

What is all this for now.

Paul began to notice how much of his life had been oriented around external markers. Titles, milestones and achievements. These were not meaningless, they had carried genuine impact, but they were not the whole story and lately they were no longer sufficient to organise meaning. Meaning was shifting toward other things. Toward presence, toward relationships and toward what he could hold rather than what he could achieve. He began to see that limits were not only loss, but they were invitations.

Limits asked him to choose more carefully. To stop scattering his energy across obligations that were more about identity than love. Limits forced him to let go of being everywhere, for everyone. They also allowed him to be more fully somewhere, with someone. Paul found himself becoming more interested in depth than breadth. In fewer conversations that mattered rather than many that looked productive. In the quality of his attention.

There were uncomfortable moments, too. Times when he felt the old reflex to prove flare up, especially around younger colleagues. When he wanted to demonstrate he still had it, when he felt overlooked and the ego tightened, whispering that he was becoming irrelevant. He learned to notice that whisper with a gentler attitude than he once would have. It wasn't wrong, it was simply afraid. It was a part of him that had organised his life around achievement and was now uncertain about what would hold him.

On his birthday weekend, Paul and Elise drove out of the city to a place they'd been going for years. A small patch of coast, not glamorous, mostly familiar. They walked along the sand in the late afternoon. The light was soft, the water was cold. Paul's knee complained a little on the uneven track and he found himself laughing at it.

"Your body has opinions now," Elise said. "It always did," Paul replied. "I just ignored them."

They sat on a bench above the beach and watched the horizon for a long time. No agenda. No need to fill the silence. Paul felt something settle in him, not as a conclusion but as a quiet acceptance.

Ageing was not just decline; it was a reorganisation. It was the gradual loosening of the need to be seen a certain way and the slow emergence of a different kind of dignity, one less dependent on performance.

Achievement had given his life shape.

Now something else was shaping it. He didn't know yet what the new organising principle would be. Not fully. Perhaps it didn't need a name. He only knew that the drive to prove was easing and in the space it left behind, something quieter was becoming possible.

A steadier relationship with himself, a deeper attunement to what mattered and a willingness to let meaning be simple, even ordinary. Not a story of ascent. A life held lightly, with enough room for grace to visit.

Twenty-Three:

Staying With Power and Love Over Time

How the relationship matures

Letter to a younger self

Dear Michael,

You won't read this now. Not because you won't have time, although you will tell yourself you don't, but because you won't yet recognise what I'm trying to describe. You are still living in the era where competence feels like love and control feels like care, where being needed is confusingly close to being safe.

You are good at things. That will serve you. It will also, quietly, keep you asleep in places where you most need to wake.

So let me write to you from further along the track, not to teach you, not to warn you off anything, but to make a small space in the future where you might one day recognise yourself and soften.

You are about to fall in love with Leila. You will call it love quickly because you will feel relieved. She will make you feel less alone in your own mind. She will listen in a way that seems to come from her whole body. She will laugh at your jokes and she will see through you, both at the same time, and you will find that both comforting and faintly unnerving. You will tell yourself she is your calm and she will, for a while, be exactly that.

Here is the first thing you will not understand yet. Your calm will not come from her. It will come from the way her presence briefly interrupts your need to organise life into something you can manage.

That interruption is your first glisk, and you will miss it.

You will assume love is what happens when you find someone who fits you. It will take you years to realise love is what happens when you stop trying to make someone fit. You will enter the relationship with a quiet belief that you are a good person because you are responsible. You will show your care through planning, fixing and anticipating. You will work hard, so she doesn't have to worry. You will think this is noble, and it is, partly. It is also your nervous system seeking safety through control.

You won't call it control. You will call it being thoughtful.

Leila will sometimes call it being managed. When she says that, you will feel insulted, then you will feel ashamed and then you will feel angry. Then you will clean the kitchen with unnecessary intensity, which will be your way of saying, see,

I am contributing, without having to say, I feel exposed.

You will learn, slowly, that power is not just what you do at work. It is what happens in a room when you tighten. It is what happens when your tone turns final. It is what happens when you decide you are right and stop being curious.

It will take you a long time to notice your own tightening because you experience it as virtue. That is not a criticism, Michael. It is simply the truth of how competence can organise the self. When competence is praised, you begin to treat it as identity. When it is identity, you protect it. When you protect it, you stop learning.

This is where power and love begin to separate. You don't mean for it to happen, but it does.

The first time you will really see it is with the baby. You think you are prepared. You are not. You have read things, planned and created spreadsheets. You will be very proud of your spreadsheets. You will also, at three in the morning, learn that no spreadsheet can hold a newborn's crying.

There will be a night when the baby will not settle and Leila will be sitting at the table with her head in her hands. You will be bouncing the baby too fast, walking in small frantic loops, trying to outrun helplessness. Leila will say, "You're not holding him right." You will hear, you're failing. Your power will tighten. Your voice will sharpen. You will say something like, "Do you want to do it then?"

In that moment, you will feel strong, decisive, and in control. You will also feel lonely.

Leila will look up at you with eyes that are not just angry but cracked open by exhaustion. "I just needed you to be with me," she will say. "Don't make it a competition."

That sentence will be a doorway. You can walk through it, or you can defend yourself and stay outside. You will almost defend yourself, your mouth will begin forming the explanation and you will feel the pull to justify, to claim that you are trying, to seek credit for effort.

Then, if you are lucky, you will pause. You won't call it grace at the time. You will call it giving up, it will feel like surrender.

But it will be a glisk.

Because in that pause, you will speak from somewhere else, not from competence, pride or fear. "I'm sorry," you will say, and your voice will sound younger than you are. "I'm scared. I don't know how to do this." Leila's face will soften. Not because everything is okay, it isn't, but because you are finally in the room with her.

That is your first clear experience of power and love re-entering a relationship. Power loosening its grip, love gaining its boundaries. Both becoming more honest.

You will miss other moments. You will miss them in supermarkets, in school meetings, in rushed mornings and in the way you will sometimes treat rest as something to earn. You will miss them in the way you will try to fix Leila's feelings when she doesn't want fixing. You will miss them when she becomes quiet and you interpret quiet as criticism.

You will also catch some. Sometimes you will feel the tightening in your chest and you will recognise it for what it is, a reflex, not a truth. Sometimes you will stop mid-sentence and choose a softer tone, not because you are trying to be nice but because you can feel what your sharpness is doing to the room.

You will begin to learn something that will humble you. Love is not proved by intensity, it is proved by repair. That is not a method, it is a lived discovery that comes only after you have failed to repair enough times to feel the cost.

There will be a season when your father will start to fade. You will do what you always do. You will organise, manage appointments and handle logistics. You will feel competent and therefore, briefly, safe.

Leila will watch you and she will not interrupt you at first. She will learn in those years that love sometimes looks like restraint, letting someone use their old strategies until they are ready to outgrow them.

One day, you will come home and stand in the hallway holding your keys and you won't know what to do next. Leila will ask you how you are. You will say, "Fine," because fine will be the only word your ego believes is acceptable. Leila will not argue with it, she will bring you a glass of water and put it in your hand. Your fingers will touch and she will feel the tremor in you.

This will be another glisk, and it will be hers as much as yours. A moment when she chooses not to demand your vulnerability, but to create a place it can arrive.

You will say, "I don't know how to do this," and something in your identity will loosen again. Not because grief is noble, but because it strips away the parts of you that were held together by achievement.

You will learn that power, in the deepest sense, is not your ability to control outcomes, it is your willingness to stay present when you cannot. And love, in the deepest sense, is not your ability to soothe, it is your willingness not to turn away.

You will also learn that you can weaponise love, and you will do it sometimes without meaning to. You will use generosity to avoid conflict, care to hide your resentment and humour to dodge what is tender.

Leila will do her own version of this, too. She will use patience to avoid truth, calmness as a kind of silent authority and sometimes become morally superior without realising it, and you will feel it in your bones before either of you can name it.

There will be a night, years from now, when you will argue about your teenage son. He will do what teenagers do. He will find the fault lines in your partnership and press them, not because he is malicious, but because he is trying to locate himself against something. You will come in too hard. Leila will come in too soft. Each of you will secretly believe you are the one protecting him.

Later, when the door is slammed and the house is quiet, you will look at Leila and say something like, "Don't make me the authoritarian parent." It will surprise you that you can say it, that you can name the pattern without acting it all the way through.

Leila will pause. She will feel a flash of defensiveness and a grain of truth. This is important, Michael. In the years ahead, both of you will learn to do something rare. You will learn to accept the grain of truth without swallowing the attack. That is where maturity begins to settle, not in perfect behaviour, but in the ability to hear truth without turning it into shame, and to offer truth without turning it into cruelty.

If I could give you anything from here, it would not be advice, it would be reassurance about what the path actually looks like. It looks like missing more moments than you want to admit and waking up, slowly, through repetition. It looks like noticing that power tightens when you feel afraid, and that love dissolves when you feel resentful, and that both can return if you pause long enough to find yourself again.

It looks like the smallest glisks. A softened tone, an apology without theatre or a hand on a knee when words would be too much. A sentence that begins, "I might be wrong," and therefore allows room to breathe.

It also looks like ordinary laughter, not as avoidance, but as shared humanity. The moment you both recognise the old pattern and, instead of blaming, you smile at each other as if to say, ah, there it is again, and we are still here.

Over time, you will stop expecting to get it right. You will start valuing return over perfection.

You will learn that the relationship matures not because you become endlessly wise, but because you become more willing to be real. More willing to name fear, repair and letting the other person be other, without needing to manage them into your comfort zone.

The most surprising part will be this; The end goal is not harmony. The end goal is not even happiness, at least not in the tidy sense. The end goal is aliveness, held together. Power and love in a relationship, not clenched and not collapsed, just present.

And when grace visits, as it sometimes will, it will not feel like achievement. It will feel like a small easing, a quiet opening, a moment where you realise you are no longer trying to win.

You are simply staying.

With love, from further along,

Michael

Twenty-four:

Grace as Something That Visits

Why it cannot be claimed or sustained

Grace is not a trait. It is not a credential. It does not belong to the people who speak about it most fluently. Grace is more like weather. It arrives. It shifts the air. It changes what is possible for a moment. Then it moves on.

You can prepare for it, in the way you might open windows before a cool change. You can make space, stop doing the things that keep it out, but you cannot manufacture it, and you cannot hold it captive. The moment you try to claim it, it tends to evaporate into performance.

This chapter is not a map. It is a handful of moments, each imperfect, each ordinary, each showing something about how grace visits and how it leaves. Take them as reflections, not instructions. If they do anything at all, let them sharpen your noticing, not your striving.

1. The meeting that stayed human

Tara arrived five minutes late and flustered, cheeks warm, hair still damp from a rushed shower. She slid into the chair beside Hassan and mouthed sorry, not to him exactly but to the room. She had been the chair of this working group for months. She was usually precise, composed and competent. Today, she looked like someone whose morning had run her rather than the other way around.

The agenda was heavy: Budget pressure - a restructure with roles at stake. People in the room had already started bracing in the familiar way, shoulders tightening, eyes narrowing, tone becoming efficient.

Tara opened her laptop, cleared her throat and began to speak, then stopped. She closed the laptop again, as if it had suddenly become irrelevant. "I'm aware I've come in a bit jagged," she said. Not apologising exactly, just naming. "If I rush, I'll make it worse. Can we take one breath before we start?"

It was such a small request. It could have been mocked, could have been ignored, but it wasn't. The room did something subtle instead, it slowed. One breath does not solve anything. It does not pay for anything. It does not make people safe. It does not change the numbers.

But it shifted the field.

Hassan noticed his own jaw unclench. Priya, who had come prepared to argue, felt her shoulders drop a fraction. Someone at the end of the table exhaled loudly, and a few people smiled, not because it was funny but because it was relieving to be allowed to be human before being strategic.

The meeting that followed was still hard. People disagreed, there were moments of tension, but the tone stayed less cruel than it might have. People spoke more honestly, owned uncertainty without collapsing into it and managed, briefly, to hold power and love in the same room.

Grace did not arrive in harmony. It arrived as a softening of the reflex to dominate. It visited.

Then, later that afternoon, Tara snapped at an email and felt herself harden again.

Grace was not something she had achieved. It was something she had hosted, briefly.

2. The apology that did not perform

Miguel prided himself on being calm. He had been told for years that his steadiness was a gift. Under stress, he would say, he became "more focused". What he meant was that he became narrower. He cut away anything that felt like emotion, and in doing so, he sometimes cut away people.

On a Friday morning, in the middle of a tense project, he spoke sharply to Jordan in front of the team. Not shouting, not humiliating in an obvious way, but with a tone that made the room go quiet. Jordan's face changed. Not dramatically. Just the small shift of someone being pushed out of the circle. Miguel kept going. He finished the meeting, moved on, competence restored and order reasserted.

Later, walking back to his office, he felt something in his gut that did not match the story he wanted to tell himself. It wasn't guilt exactly, it was awareness. A quiet knowing that he had traded a relationship for control. He sat at his desk and stared at the screen, the old instinct rising to justify himself. Jordan should have been more prepared. I was under pressure. It wasn't that bad.

He noticed the instinct and did not feed it. He went to Jordan's desk and said, simply, "Can I speak with you for a minute." Jordan followed him into a small meeting room, guarded, polite.

Miguel felt the familiar urge to overexplain, to make the apology sound rational and therefore acceptable. Instead, he said, "I spoke to you in a way that was disrespectful. I was tight and I took it out on you. I'm sorry." Jordan blinked, surprised by the lack of performance. Miguel didn't add a lesson, promise it would never happen again or ask for reassurance. He simply stayed there, letting the apology be what it was.

Jordan's shoulders softened slightly. "Thank you," Jordan

said. After a pause, "It did land hard." Miguel nodded. "I know."

Grace visited in that moment, not as forgiveness, not as resolution, but as truth without theatre.

Miguel walked back to his office feeling strangely quiet. He hadn't become a better person. He had simply not defended his ego.

The next week, he snapped again, this time at someone else, and had to begin again.

Grace does not become a possession. It becomes a practice of return.

3. The boundary that was also love

Asha had always been the friend people called when life fell apart. She listened well, remembered details, made soup and stayed.

Over time, her care became her identity.

When her friend Mia began calling every night in crisis, Asha answered, even when she was tired, even when she had work early, even when she could feel her own body tightening at the sound of the ringtone. She told herself she was being kind. She also knew, quietly, she was avoiding something. If she set a boundary, Mia might think she didn't care, or even worse, might leave. Asha might be less needed.

One night, after an especially long call where Mia circled the same despair for the hundredth time, Asha hung up and sat on the edge of her bed, heart racing. She felt love for Mia and frustration so sharp it almost felt like anger. She felt compassion and resentment coexisting in her chest like two animals forced into the same cage.

Asha did not sleep well.

The next day, she rang Mia and said, "I want to talk about something, and I'm nervous to say it."

Mia's voice tightened. "Okay…"

Asha felt the temptation to soften the truth into something harmless, but she didn't. "I care about you," she said. "And I can't keep doing nightly crisis calls. I'm starting to feel depleted and I don't want to resent you. Can we find another way?"

There was silence. Heavy, risky silence.

Mia said, "So you don't want to be here for me." Asha felt the sting. The old reflex to rescue rose instantly. She could have backtracked, reassured and swallowed her limit.

Instead, she stayed. "I do want to be here," she said. "That's why I'm saying this. I want to stay close without disappearing."

Mia's breath sounded uneven on the phone. "I don't know how to do it without you," she whispered. Asha felt tenderness rise again, and also something firmer. "I'll still be with you," she said. "Just not in the way that is breaking me."

They didn't solve it in that call. Mia cried. Asha sat with her own discomfort and did not fix it. After they hung up, Asha felt shaky and strangely upright.

Grace visited in the form of a boundary that did not harden into rejection.

Asha didn't claim it. She didn't congratulate herself. She simply noticed that love had become more honest when it stopped being limitless.

4. The moment grace did not come

Kai had been doing well, by most measures. They were respected at work and they were seen as thoughtful. People came to them for perspective. Kai had begun to believe, quietly, that they had outgrown their old reactivity.

Then came a meeting where someone challenged them publicly, not aggressively, but clearly. Kai felt the familiar heat rise in the chest, the narrowing of attention, the internal voice that said, Don't let them undermine you.

They responded quickly, with words that were technically

accurate and emotionally sharp. The room went still. The challenger's face tightened. The meeting moved on, but something had changed. Kai could feel it. The air was colder. Afterwards, alone in the lift, Kai replayed the moment and felt the delayed recognition arrive like a weight.

They had been hooked.

They had chosen power without love. They knew exactly what they had done, and there was no story that made it noble.

Kai didn't repair it that day. Pride got in the way, embarrassment and the fear of looking weak.

Grace did not visit.

Not because Kai was a bad person, but because the conditions that invite grace were not present. Kai had closed the space.

That night, lying awake, Kai felt the cost of the moment. Not punishment, just consequence.

The next morning, they began again, slower this time. They found the person they had cut down and said, quietly, "I've been thinking about yesterday. I responded from defensiveness, not from care. I'm sorry."

The other person nodded, wary. "Okay," they said. Not forgiveness, not warmth, just acknowledgement.

Grace did not arrive in the repair either, at least not immediately.

But something else did. Honesty, and sometimes honesty is the only opening available.

5. The ordinary visit

There are days when nothing dramatic happens and yet something shifts.

A father pauses before raising his voice. A leader chooses to ask a question rather than deliver a verdict. A partner listens without correcting. A friend stays quiet rather than rushing to reassure. Someone notices their own tightening and softens, just slightly, as if making room for something they can't name.

These are not headlines. They are not life hacks. They are not proof of enlightenment. They are small moments where power and love re-enter a relationship.

Grace visits in these moments not as a glow, not as a certainty, but as a brief easing, a sense that something more human has become possible. Then it leaves again, and the day continues, and the old reflexes return as they always do.

That is part of why grace cannot be claimed. If you could capture it, you would turn it into a possession. If you could sustain it by force, you would turn it into performance. If you could guarantee it, you would stop needing presence. Grace does not belong to the competent, to the spiritual and it does not belong to the virtuous. It visits when the conditions are hospitable.

And the conditions are simple, though not easy.

A little more space.

A little less certainty.

A willingness to pause.

A willingness to repair.

A willingness to stay human.

Even then, it might not come.

But making space for it changes you anyway, not because you become graceful, but because you become more available. And sometimes, without warning, in the middle of an ordinary day, the room softens, someone tells the truth without cruelty, and you feel that brief, unmistakable shift.

A glisk.

Then it passes, and you begin again.

Twenty-five:

A Final Glisk

Not a conclusion

It was late enough that the house had stopped making its daytime sounds. No kettle, no footsteps, no screens murmuring from other rooms. Just the quiet settling that happens when a place has been lived in all day and can finally exhale. Outside, the air was cool, the kind of cool that doesn't announce itself as weather, it simply makes you pull your shoulders in slightly when stepping onto the veranda.

I stood at the kitchen sink with the tap running too long. Not because I needed the water, but because I liked the sound of it. A thin ribbon of noise that gave my mind something to lean on. I rinsed a mug that wasn't really dirty, dried it, put it away. Then realised I'd put it in the wrong cupboard and moved it without irritation, which felt like a small achievement and also slightly ridiculous.

On the bench, a pile of papers sat in mild disorder. Notes from the day, a few printed documents I had no reason to print. A notebook open at a page where I had written a sentence earlier and then underlined it twice, as if underlining might make it truer.

I am not responsible for carrying what the whole cannot hold.

I looked at the sentence for a while, not with pride, not with certainty. More like someone looking at a fence they've built and wondering whether it will hold in a storm.

There had been a storm today, of sorts. Not the public kind, not the kind that makes headlines or requires formal comms. Just a long day in a living system, the kind where people bring their tiredness and their hopes, their irritation and their longing, and they don't always know what they are doing when they bring it.

A meeting in the morning where someone had said, with brittle politeness, "We need decisive leadership," and what they had meant was, Please take this discomfort away.

A corridor conversation where a staff member had looked at me with a mixture of admiration and resentment, as if I were both saviour and threat.

An email that landed in my inbox like a stone.

"We are exhausted." It read. It was sent on behalf of a group, written in collective language, as if fatigue were a formal position. It wasn't accusatory and also wasn't neutral. It carried the ache of being over-stretched and the faint hope that someone else could hold it for a while.

I read it once, then again, feeling my chest tighten. The old reflex arrived quickly, polished and persuasive.

Fix it.

Respond now.

Offer something.
Promise change.
I could feel my own competence sharpening, ready to do its job. I could also feel the hook underneath it, the ego's quiet bargain.

If you carry this well, you will be worthy.
If you carry this well, you will be safe.
I opened a draft reply and started typing.
I hear you. I will take this on. I will ensure…
The words came easily. They always did when I moved into rescue. They were competent words, reassuring words, the sort of words that calm a room for a moment, the sort of words that also make a system more dependent.
I stared at the screen and felt something in me hesitate. Not a dramatic insight. Not a moral awakening. Just a small internal pause, as if some quieter part of me had reached out and touched my sleeve.
I stopped typing.

I sat back in the chair and let the tension run through my body without immediately converting it into action. I noticed my breath was shallow, noticed the urge to get it right and noticed the faint panic underneath the urge, the fear of being seen as inadequate if I didn't respond with something clear and strong.

I didn't try to make the fear go away. I simply named it to myself, like naming the weather.

I want this to end. That was the truth of it. I wanted the discomfort to end, not only for them but for me. I wanted the relief of resolution, the clean feeling of being the one who had done something.

I took one breath, then another, not as a technique, just as a way of staying in my body long enough to think again. I read the email again. We are exhausted. And underneath, I could feel other sentences that were not written but were present anyway.

We don't trust each other enough to say this plainly. We are frightened of what happens if we slow down. We want you to hold what we can't hold together. We want relief, and we don't know how to make it.

I felt tenderness rise, and then irritation and then tenderness again. Competing emotions, moving through me like different currents in the same river. I stayed with them. I didn't respond immediately.

Later, in the afternoon, I met with a small group. Not a formal meeting, more a conversation that had been arranged because the day demanded it. People sat with coffee cups and laptops and tired faces. Someone made a joke about the organisation needing a "collective nap strategy," and for a moment there was laughter, the kind that is both genuine and protective. I laughed too, and felt how laughter can be a doorway. Sometimes it is how people test whether a room is safe enough to tell the truth.

Then the truth arrived, as it often does, not as a speech but as a stumble. One person said, "I don't know how much longer I can do this pace," and their voice cracked on the last word. Another said, "I'm scared that if I stop, everything falls apart." Someone else, quieter, said, "I'm angry, and I don't like that I'm angry."

I listened. I could feel the system leaning toward me, subtly, the way a crowd leans toward the person they believe can fix it. I could feel the invitation to become the container for their fatigue, their fear and their anger. I could also feel my own desire to be that person, because it was familiar, because it was rewarded, because it made me feel useful.

I let the desire be there without obeying it. I asked a question instead, not a clever one, not a coaching one, just a human one.

"What happens if we name this together, without asking anyone to carry it alone?" The room went quiet. Not an awkward quiet, a listening quiet. The kind that feels slightly dangerous because it might lead to something real.

A woman named Priya, who had spoken little so far, looked up and said, "It would mean we stop pretending we're fine." Someone laughed softly, not cruelly, more like recognition. Another person said, "It would mean we stop making you the answer." I felt my throat tighten. I didn't correct them, reassure them or take the role back. I simply nodded, letting the sentence land.

In that moment, something shifted. Not a solution, not a plan and not a breakthrough. A breath.

The system, just briefly, stopped leaning so hard on one person. Responsibility was redistributed by a few degrees. People spoke more truthfully, not all truth, not perfectly, but more than before. The conversation slowed and the room became more alive.

Grace visited as a glisk, the way embers do when you stop poking the fire and simply let it breathe. Not brightness, not certainty, just a small easing. The room softened by a degree, and the air moved again.

It did not stay.

Later, someone pushed back, someone became defensive, and someone withdrew. I felt my own impatience flare, heard myself speak too quickly at one point, the old authority sliding back in, and I saw the way a face across the table closed slightly.

I noticed it and I softened my tone, not dramatically, just enough.

"I'm doing it too," I said quietly. "I'm trying to end it. I'm trying to make it neat."

A few people smiled. Someone exhaled.

The meeting ended without resolution. People went back to their work. The system remained complex. Fatigue did not disappear. The email still sat in my inbox, waiting for a reply.

Now, in the kitchen, with the tap running again for no reason, I felt the day settle in my body. I could still feel the pull toward proving, the temptation to turn the afternoon into a story of good leadership, the urge to extract meaning and offer it back to the world in a useful form.

I let the urge be there. I did not feed it. I turned the tap off.

In the quiet that followed, I noticed something small and almost easy to miss. The absence of the need to win the day, the absence of the need to be admired for holding it well. The simple fact that I was still here, not triumphant, not defeated, just present enough to keep returning.

I picked up the notebook and looked again at the underlined sentence.

<u>I am not responsible for carrying what the whole cannot hold.</u>

I didn't believe it completely. Not yet. Belief wasn't the point. I closed the notebook and left it on the bench anyway. Then I walked outside into the cool air and stood for a moment under stars in the dark sky, letting the night be larger than my mind. Somewhere nearby, a bird called once and fell silent again.

I breathed, and for a brief moment, nothing needed to be fixed.

Just this.

Just staying.

About The Author

Stephen Duns is a CEO, leadership advisor and author whose work sits at the intersection of power, care and human development. He also works part time as a Professor of Business Leadership. Across nearly four decades, he has held senior executive roles and led organisational change in health, community services and public sector systems, helping leaders navigate complexity without losing their humanity.

Stephen is the author of *Expert to Leader, The Inquiry Habit* and *ADAPT: Change as a developmental journey*. His writing explores the developmental edge of leadership, where competence alone is no longer enough and presence begins to matter as much as performance. As a CEO, he puts these ideas into practice every day, inside the ordinary pressures where leadership is tested and where grace, when it comes, is usually brief and quietly consequential. He lives on a bush block outside Melbourne with his husband and their dogs, where he continues to write, advise and stay curious about the moments that shape us more than we realise.